DELEGATE

OR

SUFFOCATE

**A practical handbook for nurse managers as they
survive and thrive on the road of management**

By Peg Tobin, R.N.

Printed in the United States of America

First Edition, 2012

ISBN-13: 978-1479126828

ISBN-10: 1479126829

Contact Information:

Peg Tobin

8233 Howe Industrial Parkway

Canal Winchester, OH 43110

www.tobinsearch.com

TABLE OF CONTENTS

ACKNOWLEDGEMENTS

To my fantastic husband, Richard, you have been by my side for every dream I have ever had and you have always told me, "go for it." Without your support and caring ways this book would have never come to fruition. I am a very blessed woman to have you in my life.

To William (Marty, my oldest son), you have been my rock throughout this book adventure. You have held the business together while your mom went off and dreamed again. Thank you son, you make me so very proud and you help make all my dreams come true.

To Christopher (Chris, my youngest son), you approve me and encourage me. If only I could see myself as your eyes see me. Thank you son, you delight my soul and your confidence in me helped me write this book. You let me dream and for that I am blessed.

To my dear sister, Patsy Ziegler, thank you for never wavering in your faith that there was a book inside of me. It is amazing that you have any friends left that will stay in the same room with you when you start talking about me; you make me sound as wise as Newton and as inventive as DaVinci.

To Mike Cindrich, my best friend, your undying love and unbelievable allegiance has helped me believe that the time I have spent writing this book is not 'for want' because you indubitably believe someone in the nursing field will definitely grow from what I have written.

To Darrell Donalds, thank you for your dedication, without your artistic ability this book would have not come to life.

To Pam Lemasters, thank you for editing this book. You sacrificed your free time to help my dream come true.

To Ginger Reed, thank you for your prayers, enthusiasm and excitement. You got me started!

To Brett McVicker, thank you for being my 'armor barrier' and my friend. Your faith in me has been a great encourager.

INTRODUCTION

To understand this book, I think it would be best to understand how I became a nurse...

The school bell rang announcing school was over for the day. I could hear the children outside my classroom as they slammed their lockers and giggled back and forth to each other. They were ready and eager to expend their energy away from the watchful eyes of a teacher.

I erased the black boards, put away books and cleaned up my desk. It was time for me to head home. I pulled down and locked the windows, turned out the lights and closed the door to my classroom. I walked out to the parking lot, unlocked my car and put my belongings in the back seat. I climbed into the seat behind the steering wheel and placed the key in the ignition, but that is where I stopped, I could not turn the key to the on position.

I sat there listening to the voice in my head. This voice had come to me many, many times before but today it would not let me go any further until I acknowledged that I was hearing it. I thought it was God, but I was not sure. I was a new baby Christian and I was struggling to identify if it was Him or me talking.

Today, whoever's voice it was, it was not letting me move any further. I finally put my hands on the steering wheel and said, "Praise Jesus, if this is you then I am listening, if it is me, then stop the chatter in my head and let me get home." The chatter did not stop; so I listened.

This voice told me I was to go back to school and become a Registered Nurse. I shook my head and said, "Like that is 'not' going to happen!" I knew my husband and I had no additional funds, therefore, I figured it must be my voice. The only thing I could not figure out was why I was thinking these kinds of thoughts. I was a teacher and I was a successful teacher, therefore, why would I want to go back to school and become a nurse?

I turned the ignition on and headed home. Over supper, I shared with my husband what I thought I had heard. After I finished, he looked at me, smiled and said, "Well I think somebody here needs to prepare to go to nursing school." I looked at him and asked him if he knew something I did not? He shook his head. I then asked him if he knew where we had money for such an expense. He again shook his head. Frustrated, I cleaned up the supper dishes, helped our sons with their homework, checked my students' homework and went to bed.

As usual, the next morning I headed to school. Throughout the day, I kept reflecting on my husband's reaction and the thoughts I had in the car the day before. At times, I found it hard to concentrate. At the end of the day, I again got in my car to go home, but this time I looked up and said, "OK, God if you want me to go to school and become a nurse, I will. You bring the money and I will enroll immediately." Then that same voice said, "No you are to enroll now." I wanted to argue but I decided it was best to act.

I went to the local college the next day, put in my application for the nursing course. As I handed in my form, the Dean of Nursing thanked me for my interest and told me there was a 2 year waiting list. I told myself, "Oh that is why God had me enroll now. We are to prepare and in two years we will have the money for me to go to school." Now everything seemed perfectly clear.

I went home explained to my husband and he too agreed that must be what God meant. We settled back into routine and went on with life as usual.

Three weeks later, we received a phone call. We needed to get a flight immediately and come to Denver because my husband's mother had suddenly taken ill and needed emergency surgery. We packed our bags and headed to Denver. Shortly after we arrived, Mom died!

A month after Mom's death, I received a call from the college to tell me someone had dropped out of this year's class for nursing and that created an opening in the current class. Surprisingly the school had called everyone on the waiting list but no one accepted, therefore, they were offering me the opportunity to start class in a few weeks. Dumbfounded at what I was hearing, I nodded my head and accepted.

Two days after accepting, we received an inheritance check. Would you like to take a guess how much the check was for? If you want to say that it was exactly enough to pay for me to become a nurse! You would be 100% correct!

Coincidence, you say? A two-year wait turns into three months and a sudden death that leaves an inheritance that is just enough. No, I am 'gonna' go with the God Theory! When God speaks, get ready to move, "Now."

Back to current! Yes I became a nurse and yes it has been hard, but if you were to ask me what have been the top three toughest challenges, I would have to say...

1. Disengaged staff
2. Managing staff
3. Not enough staff

I figure I am pretty typical but I decided to ask 200 Registered Nurses that are in the role of a manager what they found to be their toughest challenge. Managing staff appeared in the top three, 100% of the time of the individuals that responded to the survey. This survey response led me to do another survey. I decided to ask these same nurses where they received their training as a manager. Ninety five (95) percent of the nurses that responded stated, "from the school of hard knocks!"

That response led me to do one more survey; I questioned 79 nursing schools in the United States to see how many include personnel management as part of their curriculum. The results were 88% of the schools did not offer personnel management.

So where do individuals studying to be a Registered Nurse go for help regarding learning how to manage and lead staff. I "Googled" Nurse Management and I visited several libraries and bookstores. I did discover there were books on nursing personnel administration but the majority of them were so thick that they alone should offer a college degree upon completion of just one of the books. In my search, I did not find a nursing management book with personal sharings of struggles and victories. There may be some out there but I could not find them.

I was looking for a book written by a nurse that did not expect to be a manager but ended up being one anyway. I wanted to read how this nurse survived her/his struggles. I wanted to read how they learned to walk the talk. I wanted personal experiences, practical advice and hope. I wanted to find a book I could relate to and one that would spark my imagination. I wanted a book that would mentor me. Theories and philosophies are fine but practicality is better when you are in the midst of a crisis.

I went to one of the colleges that did not offer courses on personnel administration. The philosophy of my college was nurses are clinical and that is what they will be taught. Therefore, out into the world I went with no idea what was in store for me as a Registered Nurse.

Within 4 months of graduating from Nursing College, I was promoted to Nurse Manager of a Med/Surg Unit, in 6 more months I was Nurse Manager of the Step-Down Unit and in another 3 months I was the Nurse Manager of ICU. By the end of my first year I had been promoted to three different management positions, with each one bringing more stringent demands and pressures. Why was I offered these positions? I was an RN (top of the ladder for nurses). Why did I take on that responsibility? That is a good question. How did I survive? How did I learn to "walk the talk"? "Talk the walk"? Some more good questions! I was definitely not prepared for what I took on but somehow I did survive.

Did I fall flat on my face at times? Absolutely, many times! However, with each fall I got a little wiser and eventually success did occur. God opened the doors and my "stick-to-it-ness" allowed me to succeed. As a Nurse Administrator, I had and still have a very successful career. I have weathered 17 Joint Commission surveys as manager of the team and our team earned Commendations each time and for my last 8 consecutive years as a Director of Nursing in Long Term Care, our team received "zero" deficiency surveys. Great co-workers make it possible.

"Success is peace of mind which is a direct result of self-satisfaction in knowing you did your best to become the best you are capable of becoming." - John Wooden

My nursing career started as a floor nurse, then went to manager to a Director of Nursing and then it grew into positions as Regional Nurse Consultant and Corporate Vice President of Clinical Services. As a Regional Nurse Consultant, I interacted with several facilities but did not work directly in one, and as a Corporate Nurse my responsibilities grew to oversee several facilities in several states. Amazingly, I was blessed in each spot with associates that wanted to pitch in and help make things better. Yes there were ones that were not on board but sooner or later they left the 'glory' train and we moved on without them. The more management roles I engaged in, the more I saw my responsibility as a good leader was to raise up new leaders and send them on to their own personal path of leadership.

For every new position I assumed or for each new department I was transferred into, the first few months were difficult. Staff acted out and did everything within their power to sabotage new actions taken to change the environment. I learned quickly not to take things personal and I found I could remain calm when a disgruntled employee was leaping over a desk to grab me because they did not like what I was enforcing. I even learned how to throw away "hate" mail without opening it. With time and consistency, each unit and facility settled down and associates jumped on board.

The more I reminisced how I learned to be a manager, the more I began to think maybe I should write a book from all my "eye opening" experiences. I had been in facilities that were on the front page of the newspaper when I arrived but in one year with the help of great co-workers the annual survey yielded a "zero" deficiency. I learned from each experience I had and applied everything I learned on the next challenge. I kept my focus and great leaders were cultivated even in the worst of healthcare settings. Everything I learned in nursing management I have been able to apply to my new setting. I now own a Healthcare Recruiting and Consulting Firm and the first requests I received in my new position were for me to train administrative nurses on the 'best practices' of Nurse Management. After a few training opportunities, I started receiving calls asking if we would help them find nurse managers looking to make a change. My response was, "you bet we can!"

When I was in the 'trenches' I used to get frustrated at the games organizations played with their nurse managers when they were hiring them and I used to hope that someday I would have an opportunity to step in and negotiate for nurse managers. Now I can, and we do. The majority of individuals that entered nursing are givers and givers are not the best at standing up for themselves. It took one 'not so fair' experience to change my whole approach to salary negotiations. Before I got stung, I was like many of the 'giver' nurses, negotiating was not my bag. I wanted to believe that the company hiring me was excited to have me and would treat me fair. NOT SO! Companies will get you for what you agree to come for, and if they can get you for less than your predecessor, they will.

When the door opened for me to step in and help other nurse managers receive appropriate salaries and benefits, I walked through it fast and have not looked back. And you know what? It is working out well for all parties!

Leaders never stop leading, and associates will seek leaders with integrity!

"Trust in the Lord with all your heart, and lean not on your own understanding; In all your ways acknowledge Him, and he shall direct your paths." - Proverbs 3: 5-6

Nursing leadership will make or break an organization.

Today I received a call from a protégé and after I finished listening to her, I decided I was going to write a book and I was going to write it now. I have heard my protégé's story over and over and nothing is going to stop until we who are in the field of nursing do something about it. I can either be part of the issue or I can be part of the solution. My biggest stumbling block has been my own thoughts. I have wondered if what I have to share will be of any significance to anyone. Today, I am not going to worry if anyone will benefit, today 'I am just going to do it'!

Before I go on, I want to share my conversation with my protégé. She had passed her state nursing boards eight weeks prior and now she was calling to tell me she had already quit her first position. Her sharing made me sad. I remember this young lady coming to my office just beaming because she was now a nurse and she wanted to thank me for encouraging her to seek her dream. However, today it was different, she was broken. She said she had received 4 days of orientation and that consisted of shadowing another nurse. At the end of the four days she was put on a unit with 49 residents. There was another nurse in the house if she needed her, but the nurse was on a different unit. My protégé was so nervous that after two weeks she ended up making a medication error. The error was not life threatening or condition changing. However, the family wanted her fired. The facility calmed the family and assured them the facility would give her an in-service on medication passing and make sure she would not be assigned to their family member in the future. My protégé was suspended for two days. Before resuming work she had to attend a medication pass in-service. This education class lasted 5 minutes and then she was back on the floor. This nurse was dumbfounded from the brevity of her training, but she did pull herself together to complete her shift. At the end of the shift, she gave her resignation. She told me she quit because she was not a kid (36 years old) and she was not going to work where she was not valued enough as an employee to be helped to be a success.

CHAPTER 1

You Have Got To Be Kidding Me!

"You spend a lifetime learning and an eternity owning your choices. Make the trip a good one."

I sat in a pool of urine with my left shoe hardly on and my right knee smeared with feces. I was on a hospital floor with my 82-year-old patient, Molly*, my arms were curled around her and I was rocking her back and forth. Molly was crying and I had tears running down my cheeks. I had frightened her when I pulled her off of the bedside commode as I entered the room responding to a code that had been called on her. When I lifted her up, her arrhythmic heart beat converted to a normal rhythm. It was a false alarm triggered by her excessive straining. In the rush of everyone entering the room, the bedside commode got knocked over and thus the reason Molly and I were sitting in urine. Molly's tears were from fear, but mine were from exhaustion. This was the third "code" called on my unit this evening and it was only 8:03pm. The shift began with the news that we had a nurse call off and each of us would be carrying extra patients. The nurse before me had left 8 infiltrated IV's and an open wound that had not been repacked since 11:30 am, plus three other treatments that were not done. It was going to be a long night.

After the second code, I called the House Supervisor and asked her if she could relieve me for a break. Her response was to tell me to get a grip and get my "ass" back on that floor, she was busy. I can smile now, but not then. I was horrified that my supervisor was speaking that way and I could not believe that no one appeared to care about the fact that I was frightened out of my mind. I cannot say the shift was very different from most of them. Having infiltrated IV's were a norm and missed treatments happened every day, but the codes were new. In my short career, I had never experienced a code on one of my patients, let alone three of them in one evening.

This was my first job as an RN and I was in my eighth (8) week. My orientation was five (5) days long. On the first day, I did paperwork and watched safety videos. The next three (3) days I shadowed another RN. On the last day, I observed activities in the ER. I was told all RN's would have to relieve in the ER if necessary. After my orientation, I was assigned to the Med/Surg Unit and given a full load of patients.

I loved nursing and Nursing School was fantastic. However, in my opinion my nursing school did not prepare me for real life as a floor nurse. In school my clinicals consisted of two patient assignments, and in four (4) hours I was out of there. As a hospital floor nurse, if I had less than 8 acute patients and was able to clock out in nine and a half hours, I was doing well. In school, I aced all of my subjects and slam dunked labs. When my instructor asked me in lab to start an IV immediately; not a problem! The "body mannequin prop" had veins so well defined that I could throw an IV needle from across a room and not miss. However, in reality many of the human veins I encountered needed a fluoroscope to find them.

I know the hospital I was working for was not a trauma 4 center. They were not even high tech and they did not do cutting edge surgeries. However, they were the hospital that trusted in me and hired me. I wanted to do a good job for them, but on this night and on this shift, I felt like quitting nursing and running out of there as fast as my two little feet could take me.

At home that evening, I played the shift over and over in my mind. I needed to assess my actions. Why did I respond the way I did? Why did I cry? I tried not to be too hard on myself, but the bottom line was if I did not want a repeat of tonight then I had to make a change. Should I quit nursing? Was I living in 'la-la land' thinking I could be a nurse? Why did the nurses that had been there a while act so poorly toward the new nurses? Why, why, why? The more I reviewed, the more I realized I was taking everything personal. I was playing the victim. Once I got those thoughts in line, I needed to figure out why I overreacted tonight. Then it hit me, I doubted my clinical abilities. I was uptight because I was afraid I would not know what to do in an emergency, which kept me in "flight mode" all the time. I had to find a way to increase my faith in myself. There was no skill's lab in this hospital and no in-service director that I could go to for training. The Unit Manager, who was my supervisor, had given her notice of resignation, therefore, I could not turn to her. She was biding her time.

"If you do not hope, you will not find what is beyond your hopes. - St. Clement of Alexandria

I had read a story written by Walter Cronkite the prior week and in his story he shared that he learned early on that in order to be a success you needed to be prepared. He said for every story he expected to cover, he thoroughly researched all the available material regarding the event, the background, and the major persons involved. He went on to say he did not design plans or labor-saving machinery that might permit him to skip this essential step to doing his job to the absolute limit of his ability. His motto was: There are no shortcuts to perfection.

"Reading a book is never enough to make a difference in your life. What has the potential to make you better is your response." - John Maxwell

The next day, my response to my self-evaluation was to arrive at work early. I did not clock in because I was there to prepare. I brought with me several index cards and a small notepad, both of which I could fit into my uniform pocket. I picked up my patient assignment and went to the patient kardexes. I searched each kardex for treatments, medications, procedures and unusual occurrences. If I found something I did not know nor understood, I went wherever I had to go to learn what I needed to know to do it right. I wrote procedures step by step on the index cards and then I attached them to the kardexes. If there was a medication that could cause a certain reaction I was not familiar with, I wrote that on an index card and attached it to the med sheet. I was getting prepared.

The next few weeks on my breaks, I wrote signs, symptoms and complications that could occur on the type of patients that were normally admitted on our unit. On one side of the index cards, I wrote the diagnoses, and on the other side I wrote the signs, symptoms and complications. It was a great learning tool. I brought in a recipe box and stored my index cards by diagnoses in the box and put it at the nurse's station. I started making 'starter care plans' for the typical diagnosis we admitted; this way when a patient was admitted I could pull one of my pre-made care plans and tweak it to fit the current patient's condition.

I found by taking these preparatory steps I was re-educating myself and building my belief in my clinical abilities. I was no longer frightened of what a shift might bring; I was now looking forward to each shift as a growth opportunity. What really took me by surprise was in a short period of time, I noticed the other nurses on the unit were referring to my index cards and using my pre-made care plans. I was no longer just helping myself; I was now helping my teammates. A month and a half later into my new direction, the Director of Nursing Services for the hospital approached me and asked me if I would consider taking the position of Unit Manager of the Med/Surg Unit. I nearly swallowed my tongue as I gasped with disbelief. I felt like I needed to remind her I had only been out of college less than 4 months. She said she knew, but she thought I demonstrated leadership qualities. I kept bringing up every reason this was not a good idea, but she kept smiling at me and telling me I would be fine. I finally told her I would think about it and have an answer for her in two days at the end of my shift.

William Harrison, Jr., former chairman and CEO of JP Morgan Chase says his advice to young people is to have a view, go make something better, get in in the game, care about it, and take some risks along the way. He says taking risks is very important. He further says one should not take crazy risks, but one should take risks all the time to improve and to prove one's self.

Wise or foolish? Risk or crazy risk? What should I do? I knew if I accepted this position it would definitely be the beginning of a new chapter in my life. I knew the hospital was desperate or they would not be asking a 4-month nurse to lead. However, I also knew this was an opportunity for me. I could become the laughing stock of the hospital or I could make a difference.

I told myself there are three components to an organization:

• **Structure** - how it will operate and function.

• **Followers** - those that will operate within the structure and respond to the leaders.

• **Leaders** - those that will set the tone on how they handle the issues and guide followers to accomplish the tasks.

I observed that I had established some structure within the hospital's organization with my "cheat cards" and starter care plans. The other nurses and staff were using my assistant tools and they were silently following my lead. The question remaining was whether or not I had what it took to be more than a silent leader. I reviewed articles written about what are the traits of a leader:

• **Honest** – display sincerity, integrity, and candor in all your actions. Deceptive behavior will not inspire trust.

• **Competent** – base your actions on reason and moral principles. Do not make decisions based on childlike emotional desires or feelings.

• **Forward-looking** – set goals and have a vision of the future. The vision must be owned throughout the organization. Effective leaders envision what they want and how to get it. They habitually pick priorities stemming from their basic values.

• **Inspiring** – display confidence in all that you do. By showing endurance in mental, physical, and spiritual stamina, you will inspire others to reach for new heights. Take charge when necessary.

• **Intelligent** – read, study, and seek challenging assignments.

• **Fair-minded** – show fair treatment to all people. Prejudice is the enemy of justice. Display empathy by being sensitive to the feelings, values, interests, and well-being of others.

• **Broad-Minded** – seek out diversity.

• **Courageous** – have the perseverance to accomplish a goal, regardless of the seemingly insurmountable obstacles. Display a confident calmness when under stress.

• **Straightforward** - use sound judgment to make a good decision at the right time.

• **Imaginative** – make timely and appropriate changes in your thinking, plans, and methods. Show creativity by thinking of new and better goals, ideas, and solutions to problems. Be innovative. (Santa Clara University)

The U.S. Army has Eleven Leadership Principles and in the 1973 Army Handbook it states: Attributes establish what leaders are, and every leader needs at least three of them:

---

1. Be tactically and technically proficient (be clinically and technically proficient)

2. Know yourself and seek self-improvement (you are not easily swayed to fit in and you are open-minded to being improved)

3. Know your soldiers and look out for their welfare (know your associates, know what is going on in their lives and do not let them over-work themselves)

4. Keep your soldiers informed (communicate with associates clearly)

5. Set the example (do your actions reflect what you say?)

6. Ensure the task is understood, supervised and accomplished (procedures written, training provided and mentor assigned)

7. Train your soldiers as a team (we win together)

8. Make sound and timely decisions (do not be wishy-washy; make a decision)

9. Develop a sense of responsibility in your subordinates (empower and give them the tools to be successful)

10. Employ your unit in accordance with its capabilities (observe the strengths and weaknesses of your associates and give them assignments that match their abilities)

11. Seek responsibility and take responsibility for your actions (give honor to those that do the task and do not throw your associates under the bus)

I knew I had much to learn but I knew I had the energy and desire to learn. I had at least three of the attributes spelled out in the Army Handbook. I spoke it over with my husband and he asked me, "What is the worst thing that could happen?" I told him I could kill someone. He said you could do that without becoming the manager. He had me on that one. He told me he was looking for me to say, "I could fail!" I told him, "Oh, yeah that too." That is when he said to me, "you only fail when you do not try." I smiled and kissed him. The next day I went in and told the Director of Nursing Service I would accept the position.

"With men this is impossible; but with God all things are possible." - Matthew 19:26

Lessons Learned:

1. If you are struggling with a situation, look around and take a hard look at what is happening.

• Ask yourself: What part of this situation do I own? What part can be changed? What part do I have to let go of because I do not have the power to change anything?

2. If you find you are justifying your actions or reactions, then ask yourself if your associate would agree with your justification? Individuals tend to look at themselves less critical because they justify in their mind why they did what they did or are going to do (they judge themselves on intentions). However, when it comes to judging their associates, it is different. The individuals are not so quick to get into the minds of their associates; instead they hold their associate's actions accountable at face value.

3. If you are not realistic with yourself, your motives and your abilities, then you will find it difficult to lead others. In my first nursing position I had two choices: I could blame others for my issues – after all the "other" nurses did not do their jobs completely – the "other" nurses did not run to help me and ease my burden – I did not get "enough" of an orientation – it was the hospital's "fault" etc., etc., etc. - they, they, they... In other words I could have taken the "victim" route;

Or

I could come up with solutions and climb over my stumbling blocks. Victory! Take ownership and make a difference. Improve my surroundings and all those in it will benefit.

The second decision I had to make dealt with accepting the challenge. I could have settled in and waited longer, giving myself more experience as a nurse before accepting a Unit Manager position;

Or

I could be a risk taker. I have never been one to sit back; I like adventure and I like challenges. I figured, "what could be the worst thing to happen to me? I would fail!" One cannot have growth or experience success without risking a few failures.

I took the risk....!

* Molly is a fictitious name to protect the true patient

** The year is 1985 prior to package care plans and computers at the nurse's station

CHAPTER 2

Reality Bites!

*"An open door is an invitation,
beyond the threshold is opportunity."*

My first day on the unit as the new manager, I was greeted with balloons and congratulatory notes from everyone. The night nurses had baked a cake and stayed over to share in the celebration. Then I woke up! Neither happy nor ecstatic were the proper adjectives to describe the mood on the unit. Apathy and distant were more accurately descript. It was strange how none of the nurses on the unit wanted the Unit Manager position but oddly enough they did not want to consider anyone else. Paint me "Pollyanna!" I could either adopt the other nurse's attitudes, or I could remain me. I chose me. Choosing me may appear arrogant, but the truth is if you do not believe in yourself you will not be able to instill belief in others. Confidence is a major key in leadership. If I believe in myself, I will have the confidence to do it, and then passion will drive me home. Individuals who are passionate about what they 'do' look forward to coming to work.

I was offered the Unit Manager position because administration liked my initiative and implementation of processes to improve the functions of the unit. I agree that Administration was desperate but still in their desperation they were looking for individuals that would take action and make things better. My process to improve myself and reduce meltdowns ended up as an avenue for me to leadership. Who knew "cheat" cards would be so rewarding!

It did not take long for the challenges to start. I was in my second week as manager when at 2:45pm I received a call from two evening shift nurses stating they could not come in because they were vomiting and could not hold their heads up. Yeah... I don't think so! These two nurses were not sick; they were poking at me to see how I would respond.

A non-producing unit can be much like junior high school; clichés and bullies and stupid behavior.

The nurses on my unit quickly learned that I took my position serious and my main focus was the patients. The nurses that continued to play games received a written counseling and if the counseling did not get the point across they received a disciplinary action of suspension or termination. I was nervous about standing my ground; it was not easy to sit across from a nurse that had been in nursing years longer than me, and tell them they needed to correct their behavior; however, I had to do it if I ever expected to get everyone on the unit to work together and keep their focus on the patients. Staff talked behind my back and avoided my table during lunch, but eventually the message got across that I was not backing down. It only took one true discipline and the rest of the staff fell into place; and the games slowed up and soon stopped.

After hearing a few dozen times that there was a difference between managing and leading, I knew I needed to find out why manager and leader were not synonymous. I learned:

Leaders paint a vision, they know when they have to step out front and lead and when they are to step back and let others lead.

Managers - administer
Leaders – innovate
Managers – maintain
Leaders – develop
Managers - focus on systems and structure
Leaders - focus on vision
Managers - direct
Leaders – inspire

Both are needed, but they are not synonymous.

As I digested the differences, I thought I was probably better suited for leading than managing. My years as a teacher had prepared me to inspire others to reach beyond their limitations and take risks and lead. I found I did not like to maintain, I liked to venture forward with new ideas and improve circumstances. However, my instincts told me I needed to keep my feet on the floor and my focus on what was currently in front of me. I needed to stay grounded, and help develop strong processes for this unit. Later perhaps I would be given the opportunity to inspire and innovate.

Most nurses start off as managers and then evolve into leaders as their roles in the organization change. However, there are some who remain managers their entire career. Strong managers are pivotal to a unit; managers look inside a company to see how they can develop the talents and strengths of their staff and because of the strength and abilities of the manager, the Leader is freed up to look outward to the competition, see what the future could possibly hold for their organization and then strategize the organizational impact of their facility.

"Be a balanced Leader: Visible, resilient, strategic, emotional, decisive, intellectual, behavioral, meaningful."

It was for certain at this juncture of my career, I was a manager. I could not look outward any better than I could lift a 500 pound gorilla. To be honest, I could not look beyond the fact the majority of the staff on the unit did not smile. They talked negative and they looked like they were sucking lemons.

When I was in college, my husband shared there was an older man that sat on his front porch in one of the neighborhoods my husband and eldest son passed through every morning. The old man had a frown on his face each day. Therefore, my husband and son wondered what would happen if they would beep the horn, smile and wave each morning to him as they passed by. On the first day, the man ignored them. The second day he again ignored them. However, the following couple of days, he started to turn his head and stare at them until they were out of sight. By the eighth day, the old man was sitting up in his chair as they went by and began to lean back in his chair to watch them further. By the third week, the older man had moved his chair to the side walk and was waiting for them. On the fourth week, when my husband beeped the horn and my son waved, the old man sat up and waved back with a big smile on his face. To this day, our son remembers that old man and shares that lesson with his children. My husband and son never stopped and introduced themselves to the older gentleman; their relationship remained for years a beep, a smile and a wave. With that remembrance, I thought perhaps applying a smile on my face might be a good place to start. Therefore,

Memo to self: "Put a smile on your face no matter what!"

There were definitely days I did not feel like smiling, but I did it anyway and soon others did start to smile back. However, I must admit, the smiles first came from other departments before they finally arrived on our unit.

I developed a name for the person I was becoming (one who accepts positions knowing they are going to have to go on to a unit or go to a facility and enforce procedures and mix things up) and it was the "Re-organizer." Re-organizers upset the norm, cause discomfort for existing staff and are unpopular; and for a military child who attended 10 schools in 12 years of schooling, this was an odd choice for me! As a child, at each new post, my first goal was to make friends. I did not care about my grades; I only cared about having friends and OMG not having to eat alone at the lunch table. Now here I was choosing to put myself in a position where warm fuzzies were not going to come flying my way any time soon. What a hoot! Life takes many turns and some of those turns can surprise the socks off of you. I figured I must have had a brain 'fart' on the day I said yes to being the nurse manager!

I would highly recommend if you are someone who is thinking of taking on the role of a "re-organizer," you not be a person who needs a lot of validation from co-workers. If you doubt yourself and your decisions, this is not the job for you.

A Re-organizer needs a strong foundation. It is a necessity to survive. If you are not married, or you are not in a solid and supportive marriage, I suggest you find a friend that will reaffirm you and be your sounding board. By sounding board, I do not mean a spouse, family member or friend that will tell you what you want to hear. I mean someone that will truly listen and help you stay on the right course. Knowledge will keep you from swaying and strong character will give you strength to stand firm when challenged.

Challenges usually come wrapped in fear and after I was knocked on my knees a few times, I learned that when I began to get a certain 'tight gut' feeling, I needed to start thinking the opposite way and then act. It took me time and experience but eventually I figured out fear is nothing but a lack of knowledge.

Step Two: without a doubt has to be:

• Make friends outside of work

• Do activities outside of work that will keep you emotionally grounded

• Read and learn

When you start managing a unit/facility/clinic, you might want to:

1. Look at every process to see if it is working.

2. Ask a lot of questions on things that are not set up and are not self-explanatory

3. Improve what you can quickly that is not working, set up goals to work on the things that will take time. Put deadlines to each one of those objectives

4. Communicate and define every player's responsibilities, without responsibilities there is no accountability.

5. Write things down clearly. Write it as many times as it takes to get everyone on the team on the same page. The written word is seldom misunderstood but sometimes you have to find the understandable language. When you want staff to see an apple you do not want to say fruit and leave it at that... Some will see an orange and think they are correct because an orange is a fruit.

6. Read and study everything. Self-improvement is a sign of a good leader.

Step Three: Reduce the fear attached to challenges through knowledge and action

Step Four: Think as a leader

Realize:

1. You are no longer the floor nurse, you are in administration.

2. It is not your responsibility to work the floor, it is your responsibility to make sure there is enough staff hired to work the floor.

3. It is not your responsibility to prove your clinical abilities; it is your responsibility to make sure the floor nurse is able to perform clinically.

Step Five: Learn your responsibilities to learn your directives. Know your position, responsibilities and the top ten (10) priorities of your job description.

An example of a list of responsibilities for a Unit Manager might be:

• Proper care delivery to all patients on the unit

• Daily activities of the unit

• The staffing of all personnel on the unit

• Disciplinary activity of staff on the unit

• Operating within budgetary constraints

• Implementation and accountability of Joint Commission Standards/State Survey

• The quality assurance process

• The timeliness of discharging patients

• Infection control of the unit

• Educational requirements for the staff on the unit

Keep your focus. Evaluate your current abilities and ask yourself:

1. What do I bring to the table?

2. What do I need to develop?

Step Six: Add to the team by hiring and promoting staff for their strengths and for what they bring to the table to address the needs of the unit. Surround yourself with those who can complement your strengths and carry your weaknesses. This is called a team! No one person can do all positions. Analyze your strengths! If you are:

• Social; hire someone more quiet

• Not outgoing; you need to hire someone more social

• Analytical; hire someone that is more a doer

• Etc.

Lessons learned:

As a new unit manager I had two choices:

• I could walk away and say the nurses are non-cooperative and do not respect me.

• I could believe I would never be able to make a difference.

• I could blame administration for putting me in a position where I had no training; therefore, setting me up for failure. Go the "victim" route;

> Or

• I could walk through the door of opportunity and have faith in myself and my abilities to learn.

• I could take ownership and make a difference.

• I could accept my surroundings as they were; or I could accept a vision of what the surrounding could be.

• Success and Victory!

Things to know:

1. Leaders are not born, they develop.

2. Leadership can be learned and developed into a fine skill.

3. Leadership exists at every level of a position.

4. All leaders do not have to be Charismatic but they all must be Credible.

5. Manipulation never works in leadership.

6. The growth of a unit will never grow any higher than the belief of the leader.

7. Leadership comes at a cost (personal change, time, money, friendships, options and freedom).

Policy Developer

This is what you will have to become: You will have to establish the ethical framework within an organization. This will demand a commitment to live and defend the climate and culture you want to permeate your unit. What you set as an example will soon become the rule just as, unlike knowledge, ethical behavior is learned more by observing than by listening. Your standards will create a trust and openness in your associates and will help guide them to fulfill the vision.

Coach

Another thing you will become: Your goal will be to teach, train and coach associates to success. A teaching spirit will make for an exciting work-place environment. As your associates are learning, make sure you are developing yourself with new information. Be a coach and show your associates that you want to help them improve and succeed. Do not be afraid to take risks and encourage your associates to do the same. It is important for your associates to know that learning by mistakes will always result in a win-win situation.

Unifier

Very important is to become a unifier: Paint a vision and paint it so clearly that everyone can see the future through it and know that the vision is obtainable. A team going in the same direction achieves success. A unifier will be able to uncannily sense problems developing and be able to step in and set things right during those critical times. The unifier will keep associates working in a vision based environment.

CHAPTER 3

Do I Take a Parka or a Bathing Suit?

"Eyes see, what life has taught."

If you were going to Colorado in February, would you pack shorts or flannelled jeans? Some of you might say the answer to that question is a no-brainer. But if you have never been to Colorado and you have no idea what the weather is like then the answer is not a no-brainer. You would have to do some research before you could answer the question or pack your luggage.

"In 1978, my husband's company transferred him to Minneapolis, Minnesota. At the time of the transfer, we were living in Southern Wisconsin (Beloit). We had moved there from Kansas City, Missouri a year prior. After a year in Wisconsin, I thought we knew what it was like to live in a cold climate. So much that I thought we were set and I did not have to research Minnesota or do anything more to prepare for our upcoming move. Wrong! The day we moved in was in November and we did not see grass until May. We quickly found out that 20 below was a heat wave in Minnesota. Our car came with a plug that you connect to your house electricity to keep the fluids from freezing in the 100 below temperatures.

The boys would take 20 minutes to get ready to go out and play to only return in 5 minutes. After one week, we were shopping for heavy winter gear. Boots and stocking hats were a must and no one in the city seemed to care about fashion statements.

It did not seem to matter what we set the thermostat at, we still had to wrap up in snug sacks. Those in Florida laugh at the snug sack commercials but in Minnesota we treasured them. "One man's trash is another man's treasure."

Never, ever assume you know all you need to know and there is no research needed.

Going from hospital unit to hospital unit, then from organization to organization, I discovered the faces of the staff members changed, but the issues appeared to remain the same:

✓ Policies written but not adhered to
✓ Job descriptions not distributed

✓ Expectations not defined
✓ Staff not held accountable
✓ Faulty communication

HOWEVER, I did find that the recipe to get back on track did not remain the same. Each facility, organization and unit's urgent needs differed. Therefore, research was needed to find the starting focus based on the urgencies.

When I first started this adventure, my head was focused on one set of procedures. I only knew one climate and one situation; therefore, I enthusiastically forged into each new unit with ideas, forms and systems from the last unit and thought they would fit. I did not take the time to learn if I needed "A Parka or a Bathing Suit!" With experience and egg on my face, I wised up and realized God gave me two ears and one mouth for a reason; hush up, listen and learn.

"Let everyman be swift to hear, slow to speak." - James 1:19

A new style of shoes may come out and look fabulous on a lot of people but that does not mean those shoes are going to be right for all of the people. Ever imagine a 100-year-old lady in a pair of stilettos? All who have feet may need shoes, but they all will not need the same style of shoes. That is the way it is with units, facilities and organizations. All will need:

✓ Policies adhered to
✓ Job descriptions distributed
✓ Expectations defined
✓ Staff held accountable
✓ Effective communication

But all will not be designed the same.

Proper changes take time and encouragement. One cannot eat the elephant in one sitting, but with time, one can eat the entire elephant.

In order for me to understand which area to start with, I needed to get to know the unit and the different personalities of the staff. The following questions are what I learned to asked myself…What are the threats of the unit?

1. What is the rhythm of the unit?

2. What are the strengths of the unit?

3. What is the culture of the unit?

5. Who are the unofficial leaders?

6. Who is a pot stirrer?

7. Who is passive aggressive?

8. Who is moldable?

9. Who are tuned-out/apathetic, disengaged?

10. Where are things stored?

11. Who keeps track of supplies?

12. Who does what?

13. Who is accountable for what?

14. Who are the decision makers?

15. What is the experience level of each staff member?

16. What is the uniqueness/talent/strength of each staff member?

Finding out what the strengths of the unit/facility is extremely important because a good manager/leader will want to find something up front to brag about regarding the staff and the unit.

After I obtained the answers to the above questions, my next move was to make sure the staff knew I knew their successes: Do not brag generically. Be specific and real. Staff can smell a "fake" a mile away. If you lie to your associates, they will never have faith in you as a leader.

'A big piece of advice'… when you take over as the manager of a troubled unit or facility, DO NOT ASK THE STAFF WHAT IS WRONG! FIRST ASK ABOUT THE PATIENTS OR RESIDENTS. YOU WANT TO ESTABLISH YOUR PRIORITIES UP FRONT.

• At the first meeting you have with staff, instead of making promises you have no idea you can keep, ask them to tell you what type of patients are normally admitted.

• If you are in a nursing home, ask the staff:

1. What is the average age of the residents?

2. What are the most common diagnoses of the residents?

3. What are the top three care needs of the residents?

4. To describe a normal day for their shift (you will be meeting with all three shifts)

5. Etc.

Looking at every process and assessing what is working and what is not working, takes time. However, there will always be some processes that will need to be fixed quickly (even if it means "putting a plug in the dike"), because to continue may result in a death or injury of a patient or resident.

Once you contain the immediate threats/jeopardies, concentration needs to be turned to the observation of the staff. You need to see if the right talent is in the right position.

Year after year studies are conducted by multiple mediums to help the health care industry understand what contributes to staff dissatisfaction and turnover. Each study I have ever read always included one of the main reasons for dissatisfaction and turnover was "individuals are put in supervisory roles that are not supervisor material or they are not trained appropriately to handle the position" (New York University – 6/2010). The following are findings published by the American College of Health Care Administration: "Quality Improvement initiatives assume that facilities have effective leaders and managers who can create the internal process changes needed to achieve and sustain the desired external outcomes.

Unfortunately, they (leaders and managers) often lack the training and support systems that will help them to escape from crisis management, develop a vision for excellence, and create the culture changes and disciplines needed for the vision to be realized"(Position Paper, 10/2010).

A reason to be in management is not because you are the only RN left in the building or on the unit. Management is an art and not everyone is born with the desire to lead. However, everyone has a talent. As manager/leader it is our responsibility to find each staff member's talent and plug them into the position they will succeed in and shine.

A group of tourists who were visiting a picturesque village walked by an old man sitting beside a fence, one tourist asked in a patronizing way, "Were any great men born in this village?" The old man replied, "Nope, only babies." - Leonard Ravenhill in "The Last Days Newsletter"

You will inherit staff that is operating in positions that they should not be in, and you will have the responsibility to let them go, or reassign them. You may find you have RN's functioning in LPN roles. After you investigate, you may find the RN is in this role because they have been out of the industry for a while and are afraid to commit to doing RN duties. This fix is one of the easier ones; you connect her/him where she/he can get the training to feel competent again. However, on the other hand you may run into a situation where the RN is not afraid but rather does not want the responsibilities of a charge nurse. This is not as easy of a fix. An RN not wanting to take responsibility will need to make some decisions. If you decide to allow the RN to do LPN duties, I trust you will lower their salary to fit the role they are filling. The Nurse Practice Act does allow an RN to work at duties of a LPN; however, the RN will be held responsible for their actions at the highest level of their education. Therefore, if something goes wrong, that RN will be held accountable for what they should know to do as an RN. Once an LPN becomes an RN, they can no longer sign under their LPN license.

As I have said before, "Knowledge will keep you from swaying."

Knowledge:

• Lets you stand firm when you have to take action.

• Protects you from mistakes that could be costly to your license.

Read and stay current with the regulations that govern your industry and your professional license. Do not expect to go to a meeting once a year and sit in the audience and think that will be enough. Pick up a booklet, book or article and read and interpret it for yourself. You might be surprised what you will read that others have missed because they are not in your same situation. Great leaders/managers surround themselves with associates that complement their strengths. This is why it is important to observe your staff, evaluate them, talk with them and get to know them. You want your team to taste victory as quickly as possible, and having the right players in the right position will energize your team enough to be able to leap tall buildings in a single bound. Okay, maybe in reality it is to jump over a small puddle.

Complementary leadership creates balance and an atmosphere where each member is recognized for his/her unique talent. For eight years, I followed a study conducted at the University of Michigan. This study surveyed employees to see what motivated them the most to stay in their jobs. Each year the number one finding was the same; the employees wanted to be appreciated for work done. Among the other choices was good wages, good working conditions, feeling "in" on things, tactful disciplining, management loyalty to workers, promotion and growth within the company, sympathetic understanding of personal problems, job security and interesting work. Good wages each year ranked 5 or lower (10 categories). Therefore, you want your team players in the right positions so you can show them that you appreciate what they contribute to the team.

When you start to lead (I know you will find this hard to believe), but not all your staff members are going to jump on the band wagon and follow you anywhere. I know this news is a real bummer, but I have confidence you will be able to get over it. If you find you cannot get anyone to follow you after a while, then you may find you will have a problem being a leader. After all, 'Leaders' do need followers! John Maxwell (author of 60 inspirational books) says, "A leader without any followers is just a person out taking a walk."

What is leadership? Remove for a moment the moral issues behind it, and there is only one definition: Leadership is the ability to obtain followers. Hitler was a leader and so was Jim Jones. Jesus of Nazareth, Martin Luther King, Winston Churchill and John F. Kennedy all were leaders. While their value systems and management abilities were very different, each had followers. Once you define leadership as the ability to get followers, you work backwards from that point of reference to figure out how to lead. - James C. Georges (Par Training Corp)

Once you have followers, you will find there will be different stages in leadership. It will take steps to get associates on board full throttle with you as their leader.

First of all staff will follow you because of your title. This is where it starts for all leaders. It is also where the biggest staff turnover occurs. The staff is going to test you, be negative and they will doubt every move you make. Therefore, transitioning through this stage as quickly as possible is imperative.

Second; once you have been tested, the staff will start to follow you because relationships are beginning to develop. This is an exciting stage because you now know your crew better, they know you and they are seeing that you stand firm. You are not 'wishy-washy' and they are getting on board because of how you treat them and paint the vision for them. Take caution here and do not linger too long in this stage, staff will start to become disillusioned if they do not start to see things happen.

Third; now the staff is following you because they are seeing things happen and things are beginning to make sense and things are becoming easier for them. This is a great stage for the organization. System are improved and in place. Staff is seeing that the changes are good for (all) the organization. Staff is excited to try more and more. However, for growth you must keep moving to the next stage.

Fourth; Staff is now following you because they can see opportunities of growth for themselves. This is a stage of leadership that most leaders stop because it is so rewarding for them. Systems are working, processes are improved, and inspections/surveys are positive. You are helping others advance. The staff is seeing your goal truly was good care and their wellbeing. How-ever, to be the best in leadership, you need to move on.

Fifth; the Staff is following you because of who you are! This is the stage you become known for your integrity and once you get to this level you spend the rest of your career developing future leaders. Not only staff members, but other people you come in contact with, will follow you anywhere because they know you never lose sight of your ethics, morals or integrity.

As you review the staff's abilities, strengths and knowledge, here are a few points to consider as you look for the future leaders:

• Who is the person others watch to see what they will say

• Who is the one most staff members agree with quickly

• Who shares the points that benefit the unit and not themselves

• Who is listening before they speak

• Who asks for outcomes

• Whose influence is positive

• Whose influence is negative

Your observations and investigations are complete, therefore, now it is time to continue your journey.

"Knowing is not enough; we must apply. Willing is not enough; we must do." - Johann Wolfgang VonGoethe

Lessons Learned:

• God gave you one mouth and two ears – listen more than you speak

• Facilities are different, yet the same

• Seek first to understand

• The recipe for success can differ - but the ingredients are the same... Not just one style of shoes is right for all, yet all need shoes

• Knowledge keeps you balanced

• Leaders need followers

Good leaders are tolerant of ambiguity and remain calm, composed and steadfast to the main purpose. Storms, emotions, and crises come and go, and a good leader takes these as part of the journey and keeps a cool head. A good leader as well as keeping the main goal in focus is able to think analytically. Not only does a good leader view a situation as a whole, but is able to break it down into sub parts for closer inspection. Not only is the goal in view but a good leader can break it down into manageable steps and make progress to-wards it. - Barbara White (7 Qualities of a Good Leader)

As a manager or leader you will make mistakes, but if you are honest and you do your best, you will succeed. Learn to ask for help and you will be fine.

Attitude will determine one's ability to lead! Below is 20 questions put together by R.E. Thompson (Leadership) to help you evaluate your attitude in leadership:

1. Do you welcome responsibility?

2. Do other people's failures annoy you or challenge you?

3. Do you use people or cultivate people?

4. Do you direct people or develop people?

5. Do you criticize or encourage?

6. Do you shun the problem person or seek them out?

7. Do you nurse resentments or do you readily forgive injuries done to you?

8. Are you reasonably optimistic?

9. Do you possess tact? Can you anticipate the likely effect of a statement before you make it?

10. Do your subordinates appear at ease in your presence?

11. Are you unduly dependent on the praise or approval of others?

12. Do you find it easy to make and keep friends?

13. Can you induce people to do happily some legitimate thing which they would not normally wish to do?

14. Can you accept opposition to your viewpoint or decision without considering it a personal affront and reacting accordingly?

15. Are you entrusted with the handling of difficult and delicate situations?

16. Do you possess the ability to secure discipline without having to resort to a show of authority?

17. Do you readily secure the cooperation and win the respect and confidence of others?

18. Can you use disappointments creatively?

19. Can you handle criticism objectively and remain unmoved under it?

20. Do you retain control of yourself when things go wrong?

6 traits of Great Leaders

1. They surround themselves with smart people

2. They demand accountability

3. They understand the power of 'Thank You'

4. They truly inspire others

5. They are engaged in their surroundings

6. They seek out positive energy

Damian Bazadona - Owner of Situation Interactive

CHAPTER 4

Gotta Minute?

*"Without a spoken word,
time spent will reveal your heart"*

I sat in a large room with stacks of paper cluttering the bookshelves and the floor. There was a path carved out between the boxes of paper that lead to an area with a desk and two chairs. I was in this room to be interviewed for an open position in nursing administration. The interviewer was the Director of Clinical Services. His desk had disheveled papers all over the top and there was not a bare spot available. Every 5 minutes or so, someone would knock on his door and ask a question or the phone would ring and he would answer. I tried to concentrate on his questions for me, but I found my mind wandering as I smiled and thought:

Is this guy for real? How does he find anything? Does he feel needed because everyone is coming to him for answers? Does anyone here handle their own issues? How did he get to this level of administration? What is he doing here? What am I doing here?

My husband's company had transferred him again and I was out looking for a leadership position. I had been directed to this organization by a state ombudsman who knew someone that I knew, that knew someone they knew, etc. You know how that goes, it is not so much what you know but who you know that gets you the job. The longer I sat in this interview the more intrigued I became, and I could feel the pull of the "re-organizer" coming out in me. The person interviewing me was not pompous, arrogant or egotistical, he was just plain disorganized. In fact, he was what I call the "poster child" for someone who needed to learn time management. His time was managing him, not him managing his time. This Director was trying to be all things to all people. Therefore, who was in charge of his time? The one equal thing we are all given in life is the amount of time there is in one day. No one on this earth will be given more than 24 hours in a day and, unless you die before 24 hours has passed, you will get no less in a day.

I liked Long Term Care (LTC), so I thought with this transfer I would try to see if I could get a position in the field. My work in the hospitals had gained me a good reputation and I had already been offered a Unit Manager position in one of the local hospitals. However, I knew if I was ever going to make the switch to LTC, I needed to try now. The facility at which I was interviewing had around 300 beds that were spread over three levels. I thought if I could get a supportive administrative position in this large of a facility it would allow me the opportunity to learn the difference in management of an Acute Care Unit and a Long Term Care Facility. I knew I needed to be careful and not jump hastily. I had already worked for an individual that did not control his/her time and energy and it ended up with me receiving a lot of extra duties to perform. I asked the interviewer if I could have a tour, and as we walked, we talked. I found that this was the Director's first time as a Director of Clinical Services and that he had been promoted because he did an outstanding job of developing systems for another facility owned by this organization.

I decided to be open and tell him my concerns and especially about his disorganization. The Director laughed and expressed he understood why I would be apprehensive. He admitted he knew he was disorganized and he was hoping he would find a support person who would strengthen his weaknesses. I found his comment refreshing. He continued to say he wanted a person who would become his work mate, someone that would work with him and in turn he would work with them. He wanted to co-share the leadership. I decided from our talk that this was the right position for me if it was offered. A few days later, I received a call and was offered the position. I found out quickly, this Director's focus was un-selfish and humble; he wanted nothing but to make the facility a better place for the residents. He definitely allotted me the opportunity to learn Long Term Care. It was a win-win for both of us. This is a great example of how positive things can come when we sit back and listen more than we talk (two ears – one mouth). If I had only judged the Director on what I saw, I would have missed a great opportunity.

The Director was eager to get started on getting himself organized. I started off by telling him he needed to think of time as energy. If he drained his energy on small matters, he would have no energy for the bigger matters. Time Management is a necessary tool for anyone who wants to become a successful manager/leader in any field or industry.

If you cannot manage your time, you will not be able to manage a unit or a facility. Envision someone trying to clean a house but every few minutes he/she moves his/her attention from one room to the next, or a teacher teaching math then suddenly starts teaching science, then back to math. In either scenario, these individuals will put out far more energy hopping from area to area and subject to subject than they will if they stay the course. I warned the Director that the staff who approached him saying, "hey, you gotta minute?" are known as energy zappers. If he did not watch out, they would zap his energy faster than the speed of sound. The "gotta minute" guys are either wanting him to give them answers to things they do not want to look up or they are wanting to put one of their "monkeys" on his back. I told him it was OK to respond to them, but he needed to tell them "that right now he does not have a minute, but that he would be happy to schedule them some time later in the day or tomorrow when he had an opening." I wanted the Director to realize if the "gotta minute" guy used a time schedule he/she would not be walking down the hall or popping his/her head in his office. They would be reviewing his schedule and emailing him to request an appointment for one of his open spots. The 'gotta minute person' is not success-oriented. They need to get on board or take the bus to another facility.

Emergencies are going to happen and there is no way to schedule time for emergencies; however, fortunately, a true emergency does not occur often. Emergencies are the extraordinary.

Some individuals go out of their way to avoid a time schedule because they think it makes them appear removed and closed off. That was one of the Director's complaints. He thought by scheduling his time that staff would think he did not have an open door policy. I asked him what he thought was the meaning of "open door" policy. He stated it meant that his door was always open and anyone at any time could approach him. Then I asked him how he thought he could ever schedule anything if he could be interrupted at any moment by anyone on a non-emergent basis. Then I asked him to indulge me for a moment and ask himself if "open door" could mean that staff could bring anything to him! No subject would receive a closed door. However, he would be following a schedule providing open spots for staff to come to him outside of emergencies.

The Director had never thought of open door policy in that light. It got him to thinking. Now that his mind was a little more receptive, I asked him to consider what types of questions, situations and issues were being brought to him:

- Were they true grievances?

- Were they requests for his intervention patient/resident emergency?

- Were they requests for him to resolve their issues?

- Were they requests for him to take on their issues?

- Were they having him think through the process for them?

- Were they asking him to do something that they should know how to do?

The Director needed to evaluate what part of the interruption he should own and what part of the interruption his staff should own. I asked the Director how, if he solved all the issues for everyone, anyone was ever going to get the opportunity to shine. I did not want to sound preachy; so, I asked the Director if he would try one exercise. I told him this exercise could snow ball into a bigger effect and result in him not looking like he closed his door but opened a door for success for his staff members. He was willing and eager to get started.

Step One: I asked him to obtain a calendar:

- Put in all the meetings that were "a must" for him to attend.

- Now put in the amount of time needed for each meeting.

- How many department directors reported to him?

Next Step:

- Go back to his calendar and block off a specific amount of time every week with each department director (realizing each director would not need the same amount of time).

• Now prepare an outline of what would be discussed and what he would expect each director to bring to each meeting.

• Send this form to his directors to have them review it and if they wanted to add a subject, to do so and return the form to him.

• Once it was decided by both that the form was complete, then that was the form to be brought to each meeting. At the bottom of the form would be space to put the areas that needed to be investigated and reviewed by the next week.

Step Three:

• Start the meetings.

• Close the door, do not answer the phone. Do not allow interruptions (unless it is an emergency, which you should come up with a code name so each would know this interruption is an emergency).

This was a small step in the Director's eyes, but it would turn out to be a big energy saver for him. The meetings with each department director included establishing special time for each of them. The Clinical Director was giving them his undivided time and attention. In these meetings, the Clinical Director kept to the questions on the approved form but he did "open the door" for any type of issues the department directors needed to discuss. The Director gave his support to the department directors and encouraged them to take control and responsibility for their department. The understanding was given that the Clinical Director would in the future redirect any staff member from that department back to the director of that department and he would only work through that director to the staff. He was empowering staff. This technique not only gave the Director of Clinical Services more time in the day (to do something like organize his office) but it improved communications between the department directors and their staff.

The feedback from the department directors (after two weeks) indicated they liked being more in the loop with their staff instead of feeling like the staff was going around them to the Clinical Director. The directors expressed they liked most knowing that every week at a specific time they would have the complete uninterrupted attention of the Clinical Director. Because staff members were not fighting against each other for the attention of the Clinical Director it resulted in fewer interruptions for the Clinical Director throughout the day.

Moving forward, the Clinical Director expanded the use of his calendar and included dates for staff evaluations (30, 60, 90, annual), dates of staff birthdays, dates of notable anniversaries (marriage, work, etc.), interviews, etc. He purchased a stack of cards for all occasions and kept them in his desk. Nowadays computers notify you on your cell phone of a special occasion a few days ahead so the leader can save energy by not scrambling around at the last minute. Computers, phones, and all sorts of technology are great tools to help a leader be more efficient.

Energy management is not complicated, but it does take discipline. You have to prioritize your day every day by what must be handled and by the importance of the issues. You prioritize in the morning and then before you leave in the evening, you prioritize your next day. As you accomplish a task, check it off with a big mark, it will feel good making that big check mark. At the end of the day, count your accomplishments and celebrate your successes. If you make your priority list for the next day in the evening before you leave, it will help empty your mind of work issues and let you begin to refocus your attention to your family and loved ones.

"It was character that got us out of bed, commitment that moved us into action, and discipline that enabled us to follow through." - Zig Ziglar

A big pitfall with energy schedules is when the individual puts down too many tasks to be accomplished in a day. Too many tasks will lead to frustration and self- doubt. Be realistic! You will have goals that will take months to accomplish but each day you may have as a task to spend 30 minutes on that goal. For this Clinical Director to make a goal to clean his office in one day would have been foolish and self-defeating. Taking it a little at a time prevented him from burning out on a "not so desirable" job. The job did get accomplished and there definitely was a celebration. I have learned to keep my task list to 3 or 4 a day. There are days I do not accomplish more than 1 or 2, but on an average I do complete 3 or 4. Therefore, I handle the few days of 1 task with humility and acceptance. To tell the truth, there are days I absolutely blow my whole schedule and do nothing. Yes, I pay for it later, but a "hooky day" can be sooooo... worth it. The 3 or 4 tasks that I am talking about are beyond the routine things a nurse manager must do (attend stand-up meetings, infection control meetings, fall, wounds, admissions, interviewing, evaluations, etc.). All meetings and in-services should appear on your schedule and as I told the Clinical Director, an important point is to re-member to mark how long these meetings should last and stick to the schedule.

Helpful hints:

a. If it is supposed to be a quick and brief meeting - have everyone stand.

b. A quality assurance meeting - bring no food.

c. Wound, weight, infection control, etc. meetings - have a format and stick to it.

The idea I am trying to relay is as a manager/leader you need to take a look at your day, your goals and your projects and think what you must get done that day. Make a schedule, post it on the facility calendar or computer and leave open times for unscheduled events. Unscheduled times allow staff accessibility to you and preserves the "open door" policy for the organization. If all the directors use their schedules and everyone has accessibility to them, then staff will start looking to see when you are available and request time with you instead of stopping you in the hall with "hey, you 'gotta' a minute?"

"The foundation of excellence lies in self-control." - H.L. Baugher

Example of the 4 Quadrants used for Energy Management
(Stephen Covey)

	Urgent	**Not Urgent**
Important	**1** • Crises • Pressing Problems • Deadline driven projects • Medical emergencies • Other true emergencies	**2** • Preparation • Prevention • Values clarification • Planning • Relationship building • True re-creation • Personal Growth
Not Important	**3** • Interruptions, some phone calls • Most emails • Some meetings • Many pressing issues	**4** • Busywork • Some phone calls, emails • Time wasters • Escape activities • Excessive TV

Take your tasks and goals for the day and put them into the quadrant they belong. This exercise will help you with prioritizing.

80% of the population spends 80% of their time in Q4 when they should be in Q2 - Stephen Covey

Nurse Managers tend to stay in Q3. The manager is a nurse, therefore, they justify every interruption from the floor as important and therefore, they think they need to drop everything and go help. As the manager, we have already discussed that there needs to be a shift in the way you think. As a Nurse Leader, your responsibility is to make sure the unit or facility works efficiently and that means the nurse on the floor is trained to handle a crisis on the unit. That is not your responsibility! It is the Unit Nurse's responsibility! Every patient/resident issue is not an emergency. Even if it is an emergency, the nurses and staff on the floor should be able to handle the situation without the Manager/Leader. When you are able to observe and let the staff perform then you have achieved true success. Let them do their job so they can shine. It is called Empowerment.

Did I do this stuff correct right off the bat? "Heaven's no!" I was going to be the hero, super nurse, invincible, etc. I could do all things! I was not as disorganized as the Director of Clinical Services, but when it came to wanting to rush to every code, I was just like him. After a slap in the head with reality, I learned to let go and empower.

If you carry a baby all the time, they will never walk.

Examples of the Pareto Principle: The 20/80 Principle

Time - 20 percent of our time produces 80 percent of the results. Counseling - 20 percent of the people take up 80 percent of our time.

Reading - 20 percent of the book contains 80 percent of the content. Job - 20 percent of our work gives us 80 percent of our satisfaction. Speech - 20 percent of the presentation produces 80 percent of the impact

Donations - 20 percent of the people will give 80 percent of the money.

Leadership - 20 percent of the people will make 80 percent of the decisions Picnic - 20 percent of the people will eat 80 percent of the food.

If you schedule your time and reserve your energy, you will be one of the 20% of the leaders that attain superior success. If you want to decrease the complexity in your life and increase your production, then you need to focus on and do more of what you do 20% of your time and focus less on what you do 80% of your time.

Whenever you start – give it your best. The opportunities are there to be anything you want to be. But wanting to be someone isn't enough; dreaming about it isn't enough; thinking about it isn't enough. You've got to study for it, work for it, fight for it with all your heart and soul, because nobody is going to hand it to you. - General Colin Powell

Managing your time and your energy is a start and this step is important in order to accomplish organization. Organization will open the door for you to move on to other details of management such as writing objectives; mission statements; writing and painting the vision for your staff; and very importantly, what duties are your duties and what duties should be delegated.

Lessons learned:

1. Control your time or let your time control you.

• Do not waste your time on "zappers." "Gotta minute" guys will rob you of your energy and take you down the path to nowhere.

• Take the time to organize your day. It is like a diet, if you take the time to plan your meals you will succeed because you will limit your exposure to impulse eating. Organize your day and you will limit your exposure to impulse meetings.

• Organization opens the door to move on and focus on other areas to be developed.

All of us are given 24 hours in a day; spend it well or forever it will be gone…

The following questions will help you decide if you are reproducing other leaders through your influence as a leader:

1. Do you lean toward developing others or doing things yourself?

2. If you do not mentor well or consistently, what are some of the reasons?

3. Have you been personally mentored by someone?

4. Do you currently have a mentor? If so, what have you learned from your mentor in the last six months that you apply to your life today?

5. Would others in your organization consider you a good mentor?

6. Does mentoring others fulfill or frustrate you?

Can you list the names of those who would consider you their primary mentor, and who have gone on to mentor others?

CHAPTER 5

Why in heaven's name am I doing what I am doing?

"Buying the material before you can visualize the product is like spending money on Oceanfront Property in Arizona!"

Why! A simple three letter word! If you cannot answer it, then you are at a train station waiting for your ship to come in. Without knowing why you do what you do, your passion will soon fizzle and you will be left feeling drained and asking yourself why you went down this path.

I have read and heard about 10 year olds who have written their purpose and vision down on paper, taped it to the bathroom mirror and by the time they were 20 they had accomplished their purpose in life and made their vision a reality. When I was age 10, my mom could barely get me to clean the bathroom mirror, let alone write anything down on paper and tape it to the mirror.

I spent the majority of my young life existing, kind of like the grasshopper; I played and did not invest in my future. When my high school counselor met with me before graduating and asked me what my mission was in life. I paused and looked at her and asked, "What do you mean?" She rephrased and asked, "What do you hope to do in your life?" "Oh," I replied, "get married, have children and stay home and take care of my husband and children." My counselor smiled at me and told me I had made a wise choice. As I look at things retrospectively, I must have appeared to be a real simpleton to my counselor. I did know in high school that I wanted to get married and have children but the only reason I said that was because I did not have faith in my ability to do anything outside of that arena. I did not believe I had the correct mind set for success outside of marriage. Man was I wrong! I should have figured that a strong-willed young lady would eventually wake up and change her life.

Moving every two years was hard, just as I was getting accepted by my peers, I had to pull up stakes and start all over again. I loved my dad and I appreciated him, especially getting to live in foreign countries and learn different cultures but he never liked to stay in one place too long. My mother's world revolved around taking care of my dad. I had an older sister (18 months) and she was my best friend. Without my sister's support and encouragement in my life, I am certain I would have turned out far different.

When it came to marriage, for a husband, I wanted a man who possessed certain characteristics. Even though I wanted to be married more than anything else, I wanted that person to love me as much as I loved him; and I wanted him to shout it from the house tops that I was his wife, and if I could not have that I did not want to marry.

To achieve my vision, I knew I had to remove obstacles that would get in my way. I did not waste my time (energy) on a person who did not meet the minimum qualifications; my mission was if a young man I dated did not possess certain characteristics; I cut him out of my schedule of activities and moved on. One would have thought I had a slew of pursuers. I did not, but remember I am "Pollyanna," I believed it could happen. My "Sir Lancelot" did come along and to this day, he is still my dream come true. When I married, I set new goals. Richard, was a Navy Corpsman and he was 'lead' on a surgical team. His team was on alert to go to Vietnam 24/7. My vision did not allow me to even consider my husband may be shipped to Vietnam and not return. That was negative thinking and I would not go down that path. Richard and I did not have two nickels to rub together when we got married, but somehow we managed. We got our dishes by filling up at the same gas station and earning points to get a dish. Green Stamps were still around so I shopped where I could attain them and I would save until we had enough to get a blanket or a set of sheets, etc. Again, I never let myself think that we might not be able to cover our bills. My vision, mission and passion were set on us surviving and being happy. No negative thoughts.

I did not pay a lot of attention in school when I first heard the words and phrases such as, "know your purpose, paint your vision and decide your mission." But somehow probably through osmosis or subliminal thoughts, these ideas did get in my head to use later in life.

"The business schools reward difficult, complex behavior more than simple behavior, but simple behavior is more effective. - Warren Buffett

In Nursing, I learned quickly "if it is not written, it has not been done." No longer could I just think of things and work them out in my head, I had to put it on paper. Anything of importance needs to be written. Studies have revealed that if a person writes something down they are more apt to do it 99% more than if they do not write it down. Writing a vision, mission and purpose brings focus to what needs to be done to accomplish the vision. A very simple example, a Vision may be to have a well fed family. Then the Mission is what you are going to do to provide what it takes to get that well fed family (get healthy groceries, bring them where you can cook them and then serve the cooked food). The purpose is to feed those we care about properly. Our Vision is how we want the end result to look, the Mission is what we are going to do to make it happen and the Purpose is why we do it. How, what and why are different ways to think of vision, mission and purpose!

Visions, Missions and Purposes work together. One does not exist without the other. These items do not need to be complicated and they can change or enhance. It is important not to get hung up with writing perfectly phrased statements. Keep them simple and real. Real and relevant are extremely important. If vision, mission and purpose statements do not make sense then no one will buy into them. If mission statements are just a bunch of words that are not true, do not post them. I took a friend of mine to their doctor and as I sat with her, I noticed the waiting room smelled musty, papers and magazines were thrown around on the tables, the magazines were out of date and the bottom portions of the tables were dusty with cobwebs. On the wall in a frame was the office's mission statement; a portion of it stated the doctors "pledged to pay close attention to every detail of their patient's health." As I looked at the dust, I doubted the validity of this portion of the mission statement. How could a doctor that could not smell mustiness in their waiting room and not notice the cobwebs, truly pay attention to every detail of my health? I remained with my friend but I certainly made the decision not to personally use that doctors.

A false statement about you or your unit/facility will stand out like a pimple on the tip of your nose.

In my life when a curve ball was thrown, I chose to kick into the "I can" mode. Negativity never did anything good for me; therefore, I chose not to let it take root. I would pick myself up and do the best I could with what I had. I definitely cried when I got hit, but after while I found out no one really wanted to hear my sob story. Therefore, I needed to hush up and move on!

I am aware that one can think as positive as they want, but that does not mean unhappiness will not enter their life. Darkness will come into one's life, but your attitude will determine how long that darkness will stay.

If you want things going on in your life, or on your unit or facility to change, the change will have to start with you. My life was not going to expand beyond my family if I did not pick up one foot and put the other foot out in front of it and start moving in a different direction.

"Doing the same thing over and over and expecting a different outcome is the definition of insanity" - Albert Einstein

Conditions can change. Change what you are doing:

1. Start by taking an assessment of what you do that is not producing the outcome you want.

2. Then take an assessment of what you have, what you need, what you can control and what you cannot control.

3. Realism will tell you what you can afford to do and what you will have to give up.

4. Once your assessment is done, then vision yourself how you want to be.

5. Break things down into steps, you need to know what has to be accomplished to attain your vision. Make certain to mark who will do what step and put a time limit on when the steps need to be accomplished.

6. The purpose should be clearly printed on paper and taped to your mirror with that vision and mission (yea, I finally caught up with the 10 year old).

7. Your purpose will be that strong ache deep down inside of you that 'is' the passion that drives you forward.

"The Lord answered me and said: Write the vision; make it plain on tablets, so that a runner may read it." - Habakkuk 1: 2

To be a Leader you need to take the time to know yourself and find out for certain your driving force and your passion. Once you have those components in focus then you will be able to lead others to find their passion. Knowing how to write your vision, mission and passion for your personal life teaches you how to do it for anything that will occur in your life.

Now that your life is in order and your vision for your life is clear, we will focus back to your unit or facility. Earlier I stated if it is not written it is not done, now I want to add to that statement: if it is not written clearly someone will do it another way.

Therefore:

• Paint a vision through communication and the written word

• Participate as a team to articulate the mission and vision

• Have all communicate their purpose

• Write the mission and post it where it is visible by all

• Meet, evaluate, tweak, reset and go at it again

• SUCCESS WILL BE ACHIEVED

As a leader, if you fail to properly articulate what it is that is truly needed to be attained; it cannot become a reality because it stays inside your head. If the vision stays in one's head, 99% of the people will not act upon it, because it is not written.

"Where there is no vision, the people perish." - Proverbs 29:18

The definition of Vision is the desired or intended future state of an organization or enterprise in terms of its fundamental objective and/or strategic direction. Vision is a long term view, sometimes describing how the organization would like the world in which it operates to be. For example a charity working with the poor might have a vision statement which reads, "A world without poverty."

A Vision Statement should inspire those around by painting a picture of how it wants to appear to the world. The Vision Statement concentrates on the future. It is a source of inspiration that provides a piece of clear decision-making criteria. To write a Vision Statement, ask yourself:

1. How do I want our unit or facility to appear to others?

2. What do I want to accomplish on our unit or in our facility for the world to see?

3. Who can help us?

4. Who can hinder us?

Your Vision Statement should be:

1. Positive.

2. Present tense (as if it has already occurred).

3. Be descript but not too robust… you do not want to lose the point in the midst of unnecessary words.

The Mission Statement is the fundamental work of an organization. It helps define the Vision and explains what you do.

1. Where do you want to go?

2. What do we do better than anyone else?

3. What will you need to get there?

4. What steps are you going to take to get there?

5. What are you going to do to convince the world 'we are what our vision states..!'?

6. The Mission Statement is the "what" and not the "why" of the organization.

7. It talks about how you work in order to make the Vision a reality.

Your Mission Statement should be:

1. Purpose driven.

2. Positive.

3. Results orientated.

4. Short and to the point – how you do it.

The Purpose Statement is the "Why" you do what you do. The core to the whole process! The Purpose is the center of everything and the reason you get up and come to work. The definition of Purpose is simple; it is "intention." Purpose is the driving force. Without Purpose nothing exists. You cannot have Vision (how) or Mission (what) without Purpose (why).

Your Purpose Statements should be:

1. Why you are doing what you are doing.

2. Plain and understandable.

3. Real to you.

4. Positive and energizing.

Purpose Statements are:

1. Your cause, your belief.

2. They explain why your unit or facility exists.

3. Why you get out of bed every morning.

4. Explain why anyone should care.

Vision, Mission and Purpose work together, they are not separate or silos. They work to successfully integrate and create a foundation for success.

In the book Start With Why, Simon Sinek states that the reason Apple Computers are so successful is because they sell their "WHY" to the public instead of the "WHAT" it can do, which is what their competitors focus on more.

"Apple, unlike its competitors, has defined itself by WHY it does things, not WHAT it does. It is not a computer company, but a company that challenges the status quo and offers individuals simpler alternatives. Apple even changed its legal name in 2007 from Apple Computer, Inc. to Apple Inc. to reflect the fact that they were more than just a computer company. Practically speaking, it doesn't really matter what a company's legal name is. For Apple, however, having the word "Computer" in their name didn't limit WHAT they could do. It limited how they thought of themselves. The change wasn't practical, it was philosophical." Perhaps you are saying to yourself right now that you just do not have time to get wrapped up with all this writing vision, mission and purpose stuff. The Company or Organization you work for has already written everything. It is good that you work for a company that has put together their Vision, Mission and Purpose, but:

• Were you part of the writing and formulation of the Vision, Mission and Purpose?

• Is it possible to make it more personable to have a Vision, Mission and Purpose formulated by your unit staff or facility staff as an addition to the Company's?

• Would it become more personal if you include your Purpose for why you work for this organization?

• Is it possible the Company you work for could use some more definition as to WHY you and your staff do what they do?

Unless you buy into "WHY" and express yourself to your associates, your staff will not buy into the Purpose of the facility or unit or you.

When I started on a new unit or with a new organization, I simultaneously, along with assessing the situation, started stating my purpose for being there with them. I let associates know WHY I cared to be there and WHY I cared to be a part of their team and make a difference. Then I would start to paint my vision, HOW we looked in my eyes (Vision) and WHAT we were going to do to get there together as a team (Mission).

Leaders are cheerleaders, if your rally the team, they will follow. However, no one wants to follow without knowing the leader has a road map.

Peg: "Hey, let's go on a trip!"
Richard: "OK, where are we going?"
Peg: "I don't know, let's just get in the car and go."
Richard: "OK, that sounds like fun."

Sure the trip sounds fun until we get a flat tire and we do not have any idea where to go to get it fixed, or we run out of gas and we do not know how far we are from the nearest town, or we are hungry, etc. etc. Spontaneity may sound exciting but the bubble will burst as soon as reality sets in with a real need. Same goes for work. A Nurse Manager can fly by the "seat of their pants," but as soon as a real need appears, trouble sets in and so does discord and discontentment. It is wiser to have plans.

Lessons learned:

1. Vision defines the "How" you do! How does it look and feel?

2. Mission defines the "What" you do!

3. Purpose defines the "Why" you do it!

Write it and it happens. 99% of what is written happens! Organizations who write down their Vision, Mission and Purpose achieve success. Make your efforts worthwhile and a success...write it down! Go the extra mile.

4. The leader is the one that others rely on to figure out where to go from where they are now! Leaders actively display "Forward Looking" traits. The Leaders direct and start in motion the Vision, Mission and Purpose

Leaders with "Forward Looking" traits:

• Take "risks" (there is that risk thing again) and are bold. They are not afraid to speak what they dream. They do not worry it may not come to fruition because they are determined and competent.

• Do not spend too much time in "today." They empower staff so they, the Leader, can work on tomorrow.

A leader can capitalize on the "why" of their associates and work them hard, but after a while if the associates cannot see a movement that has an end to the purpose, they will lose faith in the leader. The staff/associates will draw within themselves and only do what they can control until something better comes along.

Do you have the profile of a leader? (John Maxwell- Leadership)

1. Do you have influence?

2. Do you have self-discipline?

3. Do you have a good track record?

4. Do you have strong people skills?

5. Do you have the ability to solve problems?

6. Do you not accept status quo?

7. Do you see the big picture (have the vision)?

8. Do you have the ability to handle stress?

9. Do you have a positive spirit?

10. Do you understand people?

11. Are you free of personal problems?

12. Are you willing to take responsibility?

13. Are you free from anger?

14. Are you willing to make changes in yourself and in circumstances?

15. Do you have integrity?

16. Do you have the ability to see what needs to be done next (mission)?

17. Do people follow your leadership/direction?

18. Do you have the ability and desire to keep learning?

19. Are people drawn to you?

20. Do you have a good self-image?

21. Are you willing to submit to and serve others (passion)?

22. Do you have the ability to 'bounce back' when problems arise?

23. Do you have the ability to develop other leaders?

24. Do you take initiative?

CHAPTER 6

What do you mean I am supposed to empty the trash?

"Knowing is the beginning, owning is Leadership"

My youngest son was in the 10th grade and he had brought home his quarterly report card. On his report card he had a D- in Chemistry. I told him he was grounded from his car until he raised his grade in Chemistry. The next grading period arrived and my son was on the front porch to greet me when I got home from work. He was smiling and giving me the thumbs up. When I got out of the car, he came over, handed me his report card and put his hand out, palm up and said, "Okay, hand over the keys." I was excited for him. I quickly reviewed his report card and as I found his new score, I looked at my son and said, "Christopher, when I said raise your grade, I meant more than taking it from a D- to a D." Christopher looked at me, smiled and said, "Hey, you said raise it, I did, give me the keys."

Christopher was 100% correct. I had not been specific with him as to what I meant by raise. My expectations were not spelled out clearly to him. I smiled and gave him the keys, while shaking my head the entire time.

I am so glad I had this experience with Christopher (even though he hates it when I refer to it in anyway), this experience helped prepare me immensely for some of the personnel dealings I would encounter as a manager and leader.

I learned it does not matter if I am dealing with one or a group of individuals; I need to make certain everyone is on the same page. Not only on the same page, but that we are all seeing the same outcome and that we have the same understanding of how we are going to get there. As I have stated before, "never underestimate the written word." I also want to say "a picture is worth a thousand words." Therefore, draw a picture or use a photograph if you need to, but make sure you communicate what you see in your mind.

There are going to be a few constants that exist on struggling units or troubled facilities. One of those constants is job descriptions not distributed. Job descriptions help build communication and draw pictures for staff to understand.

Everyone's responsibility is 'No one's' responsibility. If you do not define out who is to do what, then there will be things done once in a while or not at all.

The Government and State Organizations think job descriptions are so important that they request that all organizations in the state issue them to an employee on the day of hire. If an individual is terminated and applies for unemployment, one of the first questions asked of the employer is, "was the employee given a job description?" Usually the question immediately after the job description is, "did the employee understand the expectations of their position?"

Whether Job Descriptions are required or not should not matter to you as a manager/leader. You should want them because you want to make sure your staff members understand the duties they are expected to perform. Your staff deserves to have a guide that will help explain to them the responsibilities and parameters of their position.

Some individuals in leadership think there is no need to have written job descriptions or expectations; some leaders only hand them out to be compliant but do not refer to them. My advice is to watch out for those types of leaders. If your superiors do not supply you with company job descriptions and expectations, then "go the extra mile" and write some. These items do not have to be long and technical; they only need to be clear, to the point and understandable.

I cannot emphasize enough that you should be cautious around individuals that scoff at job descriptions. There is usually a hidden agenda with these types of leaders:

• They like to control your every move

• They like to treat you as a puppet

• They like to constantly keep you guessing

• They are "do as I say, not as I do"

• They like to shift blame to others

Without things written, a superior can bounce you all over the place and say it is your job and you have no ground to stand on to disagree or file a complaint.

I have worked with individuals that look at their employees as a means to get things done and make them-self look good. These individuals do not look at staff as individuals with strengths, weaknesses and the ability to grow. To them, one nurse is the same as any other nurse.

A nurse is not a nurse, there are many specialties in nursing and each specialty has different regulations to function within and each has different latitudes to operate within. When a nurse changes specialty they will need to be orientated to the new regulations and learn the latitudes of their new field of practice.

A Home Health Nurse that goes to work in a Long Term Care setting will learn there are no standing orders to draw from and use at their discretion. A Long Term Care Nurse that goes to work in a Hospital will learn the doctor will be in everyday to assess the patient and they will be less dependent on the nurse in this setting.

Job descriptions help new individuals know what is expected of them and orientation educates the nurse as to their parameters or latitude for decision making. Job descriptions help individuals plan their success! Without job descriptions, individuals are functioning under their own preconceptions and doing what they think they should do and not doing what they do not think they should do. Without a job description associates put themselves in a vulnerable position. Lack of order, direction, and accountability is the beginning of chaos. With chaos, unofficial leaders take over and survival mode kicks in.

Every "upside down" unit or facility I joined, I heard 99% of the time 100% of the associates/staff members say they do not have a copy of their job description and they have no clue what their job expectations are currently. How can a manager hold their associates accountable for their actions when the associates have nothing in writing to tell them their responsibilities/duties and what the ramifications are for not performing well.

Some of you reading this book may remember the story in the news about a lady that sued McDonald's for McDonald's coffee burning her between the legs. The lady bought the coffee at the drive thru and placed it between her legs and when it spilled it burnt her legs. The lady actually won the lawsuit because there was no label on the coffee cup warning the public that the coffee was hot and may cause burning if spilled on the skin. If it is not written, a person (like this lady) can come along and say, "I did not know that was my responsibility." You would think an adult would know better than to place hot coffee between her legs in the first place and second place know better than to try and drive with a hot cup of coffee between her legs. According to the judicial system, "should-a-known" is not an expectation. McDonald's had to write a warning and publicly post it so everyone would know they serve hot coffee and it may burn them if they spill it on themselves.

"Nothing in the world is more dangerous than sincere ignorance and conscientious stupidity." - Martin Luther King, Jr.

If a nurse decides to not check that all the food trays are delivered and a manager decides to give this nurse a written warning, if it is not explained as part of this nurse's responsibility, duty or expectation, the manager has no grounds to base the warning. All the nurse has to state is, "I did not know it was my responsibility to make sure the nurse assistant delivered all the food trays." The blame is shifted to someone else. Without a clear understanding of responsibility and expectations it is very easy to activate the "blame finger."

As professionals, nurses are governed by the Nurse Practice Act of their state. Their education has trained them to govern their own actions while practicing nursing. Registered Nurses do not require supervision of another nurse to oversee their nursing duties. This is not the same for Licensed Practical Nurses (LPN). An LPN must be supervised by a Registered Nurse, and a Nursing Assistant must be supervised by a nurse (LPN or RN). However, all Nurses are held to a code of ethics that does not need to be spelled out in a job description.

Job descriptions communicate to staff who is to do what and who is accountable. Policy and Procedure Manuals direct a nurse on the proper procedure to follow to do a certain treatment or test, but the policy and procedure is not a training manual. Nurses are referred to as professionals and they are required to have a license or certification to work. Therefore, when a registered nurse enters your employ with a license/certification they are supposed to be competent enough to work independently as a registered nurse.

There will be times when actions will be taken by a nurse and others that will defy all logic. It will not matter how clearly you think you have communicated with this individual or how many job descriptions or job expectations you have had them sign, there will be certain professionals that are an "accident" with a license.

I had the opportunity to sit on a nurse review board regarding a nurse that had taken a medication in the form of a pill, crushed it up, ground it and then diluted it and gave it to the resident via an IV. The resident died. The nurse's defense was she had "no idea that this action would result in the death of the resident, she was just trying to make sure the resident got their medication and the resident would not swallow." I sat in disbelief as I listened to this nurse. "She had no idea that this action would result in a death?" If she had no idea what she was doing then why was she doing it? She was a nurse not a pharmacist! It was her responsibility as a trained nurse to know the consequences of her actions in this case.

"I can do no other than be reverent before everything that is called life. I can do no other than to have compassion for all that is called life. That is the beginning and the foundation of all ethics." - Albert Schweitzer

This nurse may have justified her actions in her mind by saying she was performing her duties by making sure the resident got their medication but what she failed to do was hold herself accountable as a nurse. Nurses are trained to know what can be and what cannot be administered through an IV.

It is unfortunate but as a nurse manager you will experience some nurses that will make you wonder why they chose to be a nurse and you will ask yourself, "how in heaven's name did they pass the NCLEX?" These nurses will leave you speechless. "Accidents" are not trainable. Fire them, report them and move on.

Job descriptions spell out duties and responsibilities. Responsibility is synonymous with duty and a key component to duty is accountability.

"A duty dodged is like a debt unpaid; it is only deferred, and we must come back and settle the account at last." - Joseph E. Newton

The nurse that performed the lethal IV was an RN and she was a Unit Manager, which means she had authority over other nurses. With that point in mind, what does a subordinate do when a supervisor or even physician requests you to do something you know or even think is unethical, harmful or illegal, etc.? Ninety-nine percent of job descriptions have a line under Major Tasks, Duties and Responsibilities that state, "perform all other duties as assigned by your supervisor." What if this nurse had directed another nurse to perform the infusion? Should the nurse do it? If the nurse did do as directed and a death did occur, could they state, 'My supervisor told me to do it!'?

This is where knowledge becomes the foundation on which you can firmly stand. Nursing Law educates a nurse as to what actions they can take and what actions they cannot take. Nurse Law states, "It is unlawful to follow the directive of a supervisor or allow a supervisor to commit an action that you know to be dishonest, immoral or illegal." It is not easy to stop a supervisor nor is it easy to tell a supervisor no, but it is your "duty" to do just that, for you will be held "accountable" for the decisions you make and the actions you take.

"You might have to execute orders you don't like, but there is no excuse for dishonesty, immorality, or illegality. Behaving honorably is your most important duty to yourself and your organization. You can't plead ignorance. You can't say, "I was just doing what my boss told me to do!" As the boss, you can't whine, "I was just following the plan my CFO or accountant laid out." You must follow your internal moral compass. As a leader, especially a CEO or a board member, you have a duty to protect shareholder's interests. And as an employee, it might sometimes

become your unfortunate duty to speak up when you identify underhanded or shady behavior." - Kelly Perdew

Responsibility and duty does not mean blind obedience. A leader assesses and does what is needed to be done and they use the strong moral compass that Kelly Perdew mentions to guide them.

If you have a nurse on your team that does make an unethical decision you will be held accountable for having this nurse on your team. Your job will be to show the authorities that this nurse did not follow protocol and stay within the boundaries of his/her job description. This is where written policy and procedures are important.

As a leader you will want:

• Job descriptions to help bring understanding

• Job expectations to help define accountability

Never lose sight of the individual filling the position. Paper compliance is important, but none the less a tool; and that tool is there to help an individual to be a successful member of a team.

"A car is a fantastic tool to get from one place to another, but you need a human being to drive the car." The car is a tool, the important one is the individual whose intelligence, compassion and morals is steering the tool."

I had a nursing assistant on our team that after attending an in-service, regarding dignity and the resident, she had an awakening. The in-service was held to discuss the fact the resident, even though they live in a confined facility, they were none the less women and men with histories and families. One of emphasis in this in-service was to ask the staff to apply distinction to each and every resident. The next day as I was making rounds, I turned onto the unit of this nursing assistant. When I opened the door to the unit, she was standing at the end of a row of 6 wheelchairs. In each chair was a female resident with their hair combed, make up on and their outfits appropriate for the time and season. This nursing assistant was grinning from ear to ear and she stood proudly and watched me assess each resident and tell each one of them how nice they looked and smelled. This nursing assistant had taken the time to make sure her female residents looked and smelled like females. I congratulated her. It was nice to see! However, there was one "small" issue, the nursing assistant had combed the resident's hair and applied their makeup to look just like her. There sat a row of 6 female residents with the exact hair style and makeup of the nursing assistant.

Do you think I made fun of the nursing assistant? Not on your life! I was proud of her initiative. She was listening and she was trying. What I learned was that I needed to tweak the in-service a little more. I appreciated this staff member's enthusiasm and I harnessed it and rewarded her.

There are lots of cars in the world and if they are in good working condition they have the ability to take an individual from one destination to another; however, not every individual has the ability to drive a car safely from one destination to another. There are lots of individuals that become nurses but not all of those nurses are able to do the duties and fulfill the job expectations on your team. Some of those nurses may only need a tune-up in order to perform to their full potential, but some may never rise to the occasion even if you do a complete overhaul.

Help your team be a success and reach their destination, write an owner's manual (job description with expectations) and give them a fighting chance. Give them a road map.

Lessons learned:

• Specialty areas require orientation and education.

• Nurses are professionals and are held accountable for the education they receive to practice as a nurse.

• Job descriptions are a tool used to help team members experience success.

• Job expectations help team members understand how they are being measured for success.

• Be responsible as a leader and do everything possible to grow your team members.

• If you do not know how to write a job description or how to set expectations; buy a book that has multiple job descriptions in it and find one that fits your need and then "tweak" it until it fits your company.

Before you can hold an employee accountable:

1. Set clear and measurable expectations

2. Include time for commitment

3. Measure progress toward success

4. Provide feedback routinely

5. Link them to consequences

6. Evaluate and give credit for their success

A suggestion:

Consider (at the end of the job description) instead of the routine statement, put a promise. I found as a manager when I made a promise to staff, my words were taken much more seriously.

Employee:

As a Registered Nurse, I promise to perform the above mentioned duties intelligently and professionally and to the highest degree of education I have received. My promise is to provide quality care to the residents assigned to my care and to encourage and assist staff assigned to my team to grow and flourish with positive comments and proper direction.

Supervisor:

As your supervisor, I promise to give you the proper tools you need to be successful in your position. I promise to listen to you without interrupting you. I promise to research your concerns. I promise to support your actions and decisions as long as you remain legal, moral, and ethical. I promise to give you credit for a job well done and to brag about your accomplishments. I promise to be your partner in the growth of your career.

"Nothing destroys trust faster than making and breaking a promise. Conversely, nothing builds and strengthens trust more than keeping a promise you make." - Stephen R. Covey

CHAPTER 7

Birds of a feather flock together!

"A tree planted in a desert is not going to be an Oak."

When I returned to college to get my degree in nursing, I was required to take a class called "Human Development." I found this class to be one of the most enjoyable and eye opening classes I ever had to take. Perhaps it was because I was older and had experienced some life and could relate to actual events that were covered in this class. One of our assignments was to observe people of different ages; the teacher had us note the actions that occurred between two or three people of the same age when they interacted with each other. One of the things I learned was the older one gets the more they tend to migrate to individuals like themselves and pull within themselves. When we are two years old, we do not notice differences; we are within ourselves and only believe in what we see at the time we see it. Thus the reason a two year old will hide themselves behind a couch with their buns sticking out and be amazed they are found. When we get to be teenagers, we are still into self (egocentric), but now we identify ourselves and our thoughts to those that surround us. We even judge our importance by the circle of friends we hang with on a daily basis. From teenage hood on we look to exist in a certain environment and culture. Meaning as working adults it is important for us to work in the right culture or else we will not flourish and be successful.

Ducks like to fly low and go from one gathering place to another; they float in ponds and hang in groups of ducks. Eagles on the other hand like to soar high and be independent. The Eagle likes to perch and develop private nests. Eagles tend to hang only with their immediate family. Therefore, if you try to put an Eagle in the environment and culture of a Duck, that Eagle is not going to flourish well and vice versa. Therefore...

"Don't send your Ducks to Eagle School" - Jim Rohn

When you start to interview for a certain position, it is very important to know if you need a duck or an eagle. This piece of information will help you avoid a lot of heart burn which can come from making a bad hire. Going into every interview looking for the same attributes and traits will lead you to hire individuals of one type. If you hire all leaders, who will follow?

Hiring 'the right person for the position' is one of the most important duties you will perform as a leader. People 'make or break' a company, therefore, you do not want to rush this process.

It took me years to get over two very bad habits:

1. If I liked you and we had a good conversation, I wanted to hire you.

2. If you were having a rough time, I wanted to hire you and show you a better life.

Through trials and tribulations, I learned that just because you like someone and you like talking to them that does not mean they can do the job. Being a good conservationist is a nice attribute; but, not if the individual tends to talk more than they perform their duties. That attribute suddenly becomes a deterrent.

Second, you cannot live someone else's life. "You can lead a horse to water, but you cannot make them drink." In the majority of cases, the individuals that are having a rough time are having a rough time through their own actions. These individuals will bring their problems to work and they will disrupt the whole team's progress. Victims are victims because they have learned to survive in that role and they choose to remain there. A facility full of victims will stay in turmoil because no one is able to see beyond themselves.

The "right person for the position' will allow all team members to do their jobs and open the door for each team member to experience success and move ahead. Failure has been a good teacher for me; it has taught me things to avoid. Thomas Edison when interviewed said he did not experience 1000 failures; he experienced 1000 ways to do things different.

To get started you must have two items and they are (1) a job description and (2) written expectations. These two items will take the emotions out of a situation and keep the focus on what is best for the unit/facility. The candidate either meets the job expectations or they do not; it is black and white and if the candidate does not meet their expectations, let them go. You can love a candidate to pieces but it is not good for the team to hire someone just because you feel sorry for them or you like them too much to hurt their feelings. The success of the team weighs heavily on the behavior of the leader.

The following are some suggestions of steps to take when you are preparing to hire for an open position:

1. Take a good look at yourself; it is good to know your strengths and weaknesses so you will be able to keep them in check when you are doing the interview. Know what complements the team needs to be more successful.

2. Be able to verbally express your management style (hands-on manager, hands-off manager, likes written reports, likes verbal reports, wants to be copied on all emails sent out to staff or managers, overseer, open-door, closed-door, etc.). You want to put it up front how you handle yourself and what you expect in return.

3. Be able to express the culture of the company (dress a certain way, speak a certain way, work hours set/not set, beliefs, expected to participate in social functions and community fund raisers, competitive atmosphere, friendly, reserved, surface, faith based, etc.).

4. Review the job description. Does it describe what you want for this position? Are the requirements ranked according to importance?

5. What kind of personality would function best in this position (for instance putting a quiet person with very little imagination into a Staff Development Coordinator position might not be the best choice).

6. Prepare 'care case' scenarios to ask the interviewee. This will gauge knowledge and decision-making ability of the individual.

7. Review the job posting before it goes to the press; make sure it states well the type of individual you are looking for this position. You do not want to be bogged down with applications that do not meet the minimum requirements.

8. Select the team that will be part of the interview process. Set up the team's availability for interviews before the process begins. Decide who will zone in on what specific area of competency with the interviewee. Ideally, you would want to include a peer as well as other supervisors. A peer will be able to assess whether the candidate interviewing really knows the position or only knows how to talk it (such as a nurse that will be doing technical submissions to health insurance companies or Medicare, etc.). I recommend that you start with one person doing the interview and, if it goes well, the next interview could be a group interview or a time to sit with others one at a time. You do not want to drag the process out too long but you also do not want to rush. The point is not to delay so long or rush too quickly that you miss getting the 'ideal candidate'.

The interview:

1. With resume in hand, start with a phone call. Talk to the individual over the phone, this will help you to access their ability to be understood over the phone and also to let you know they have a phone so you can reach them when necessary. Ask them to tell you about what their current position and what duties are included.

2. If the phone interview goes well, ask permission to conduct a couple of reference calls. This will give you an idea how others speak of the candidate before you meet face to face and perhaps give you feedback on how well the candidate worked with other peers and supervisors.

3. On the first face to face, ask them what they know about your company. A person who has done research is telling you they are also checking you out. Seek to find if they know you have specialty units, Christian-based, Jewish-based, County-owned, Public or Private-owned, total number of facilities, survey history, reputation, etc. How well have they researched you?

4. Observe their habits; how do they sit, do they wiggle a lot, do they look you in the eye, do they appear confident, are they boorish, are they chewing gum, etc. How are they dressed, observe their nails, the amount of jewelry they are wearing, the amount of perfume they have applied, their make-up, etc. These are items that give you an insight to whether the individual will fit on the surface with the company's culture.

5. In the interview you will want to ask questions that will reveal their educational, leadership and clinical knowledge.

• Have them explain further their current duties, responsibilities and expectations. Keep their resume in front of you so you can refer to different positions the candidate has held with different organizations.

• Ask them what they like most about their current position and why.

• Ask them what they like least about their current position and why.

• Ask them what accomplishment they are most proud of in their career.

• Ask them how they have held staff accountable. Give an example.

• Ask them how they handle conflict, challenges and negative outcomes.

• Ask them what motivated them to apply for your position.

• Ask them what their understanding of the duties, responsibilities and expectations are of the position they are applying for with your organization. Take the time to be specific with them about portions of the job description to make certain they understand what is being requested of them regarding performance.

• Give them a scenario that includes your organization's cultural standards and ask them for their response.

• Ask them what leadership style they work best with.

• Ask them what is their style of leadership and why did they choose that style

• Have them give you some examples of when their leadership style was successful and times it was not best for the situation.

• Give them some management scenarios and ask them how they would respond.

• Ask them what kind of quality assurance programs they have been involved in and how many they initiated.

• Ask them why they want to leave their current position

The following are general questions that may give you more insight to the candidate:

1. Ask them if they have questions for you right up front. Be cautionary if they have no questions because this can represent low initiative thinking and lack of buy-in.

2. What is your philosophy on goal setting? Is this person one who sets goals autonomously or one who needs to be held accountable for everything? Everyone usually answers, "Yes, I set goals." You must press them to find out if the goals are applicable with actions steps and follow-through. Ask them about their 'Why'.

3. What kind of reading material would I find on your coffee table, nightstand, kitchen table, car, etc.? This will reveal if this candidate is thirsty for knowledge and it will show what kind of knowledge they are seeking. Follow up question: What is your favorite professional book?

4. Tell me a story about a time you have been placed in an ethical dilemma and what happened? This reveals the candidate's moral compass.

5. How did you earn money while in college? This will reveal their drive and convictions. You will find out if they took charge of their life and supported themselves or if they continued to let their parents carry the load.

6. Tell me what would really surprise me about you? This will make the candidate think on their feet.

7. How would your world change if you got this position? This will help clarify their motivation to join your organization.

8. How do you stay organized? The candidate should be able to articulate their methodology behind organization strategy.

9. Share some stories about the four most influential people you know? This type of question gives you more insight to the candidate's culture and admirations.

10. What should I have asked you that I have not? Do they know how to close and get move on to the next step? This shows leadership qualities.

If your company, unit or facility has had a bad reputation, there probably will not be a long line of potential candidates beating down your door. Perhaps, your organization will need to invest some time in getting the word out that things have changed and improvements have been made. That may help draw in some local talent but it may be a strong possibility your organization will have to expand their parameters in order to attract 'top talent' that is willing to gamble on your organization. If your organization has a positive reputation, then the only issue you will have to deal with is competition, and competition starts with the 'branding' of your facility or unit.

You may think that as a nurse manager it is not your job to compete for strong individuals to join your team, but as a nurse leader, it is a part of your responsibility. I sincerely doubt as a leader you would want others making the decision on who to hire for your team and who not to hire for your team. If you want to make your own choices, then you have to take on part of the responsibility of how your company is going to be represented.

Some questions you may want to start with to get ready to compete are:

1. What does our company have that is attractive (flexible hours, great benefits, educational assistance, competitive salary, recognition programs, daycare on site, shared positions, etc.)?

2. Is there anything you could be doing better so it becomes an attraction?

3. Is there anything happening in the industry that you are not offering but you could?

You always want to know your market before you start to compete in it, therefore, know who you are as an organization and what makes your organization stand out.

• **Tip One**: **Identify Your Brand** - Your brand is your image. It is the distinguishing characteristics that separate you from everyone else. Your brand will speak for you when you are not present. For example, when you see the 'swish check mark', you automatically think of Nike; not a word has to be spoken.

Talent Attracts Talent - Brag about the individuals in your organization. Your organization's top talent should be involved with the community. Talent attracts talent. For example: LeBron James (NBA Star) left the Cleveland Cavaliers to join the Miami Heat. When he was interviewed as to why he chose to leave, LeBron shared he left to be challenged by more talented players. He stated he needed to develop into a better player and he could not do that unless he was around by more talented players than himself.

Exhibit Confidence - Know the attributes of your organization and be confident in them. Do not be arrogant. Arrogance turns talent off. It is one thing to know you have worked hard to attain your reputation and it is OK to be proud in advertising about it, but it is another thing to be arrogant and think you cannot stumble.

• **Tip Two**: **No Warm Bodies** - Research and know who to avoid in the industry. Let the industry know that you are not interested in 'just' filling a position. A little discomfort today in order to secure a better future is worth the discomfort. A disengaged employee can rip the life out of a team faster than a 'spraying skunk' can empty a room.

Dig deep, Get to know the candidate - Top Talent will come back for more than one interview. Show off your organization with a tour. Introduce the top talented candidate to your top talent. Have the candidate shadow a current employee. This helps a candidate see if they really want to join you and it gives your organization the opportunity to see how the candidate interacts with your staff. I realize this step is hard to do for some entry level 'Top Talent' positions, but if it is at all possible it is a good step to include in the hiring process.

Never Stop Looking for Talent - Just because all of your positions are filled at this time, never stop looking to the future. People do win the 'lotto'.

If you want a Coke, make sure you say what you mean or you may end up with a Pepsi.

• **Tip Three**: Talent Follows Strong Communication - Top Talent will evaluate you and your organization on your ability to communicate the needs of the position. Therefore, while the word is getting out from them about your organization, let them share with others that you as an organization include an evaluation on their ability to communicate in the interview process.

You might want to consider asking the candidate while they are there to explain in writing something simple that is pertinent to their area of expertise. It does not have to be a long assignment, but by doing the writing during a face to face interview, you will be able to see if they can communicate through the written word. Another idea is to ask them to describe something that is in the room and see if you can figure out what they are talking about. This shows another ability to communicate in a different form. You do not want to move on to a second interview if you cannot communicate well on the first interview.

• **Tip Four**: **What's In It For Me** - One-sided relationships never last for long. All top talent want to know What's In It For Me (WIIFM). Therefore, get the word out how a person who has top talent will benefit by joining your organization.

Investigate your candidates before you start to interview them (do references). Do a Google search and see what they bring to the table before they open their mouth. The same way a company expects a candidate to have researched them; a candidate should not be surprised that the organization has researched them. It is important for you to know the pain that is driving your Top Talent to be open to speaking with other organizations. The fact they are talking to you shows there is an opportunity to draw them over to your organization, but this will not happen if you have not done your research on the candidate.

A one bedroom apartment may be exciting when you first marry, but after three children, it is more than likely not going to be as satisfying. Give your staff what they need to function well and they will stay with the organization. Then they will attract others to your organization.

• **Tip Five**: **You want to keep them, then show them something worth hanging around for** - In order to get top talent, the company needs to own up to their brand and what they said in the offer letter and interviews as well as what they say they are to the public. Top Talent likes to entertain opportunities; therefore, an organization will need to continue to make opportunities happen in order to retain top talent. Incentives drive employees to work harder in order to obtain them; but if you offer them, be able to deliver. If you hire top talent and you promise certain bonuses then do not change the dance card.

Lessons learned:

First:

• Look at the candidate objectively.

• Do thorough references (before hire).

• Evaluate, evaluate, evaluate (before hire).

• Take your time and invest on getting the best up front.

• Invest and keep the best.

• Do your job as a manager and be responsible.

Second:

• Think through the position you need before you start interviewing for it.

• Do not hire an eagle for a duck position.

• Put your gut feelings in 'left' field temporarily while you are interviewing for the basics.

• 'Gut feelings' do come into play when the interview gets to the cultural fit arena, until that time feelings can take you down a path you do not need to travel.

• Develop job descriptions. If you have job descriptions that are given to you by your corporation and they do not touch on every area you consider important, then develop an addendum to attach to the company job description.

• Expectations give the employee the parameters they need to measure their success.

Third:

• Be transparent.

- Remain transparent.

- Be honest.

- Have integrity and do not play games. The truth will always come out.

- FOLLOW THROUGH.

CHAPTER 8

Who me?

Your dog sits next to his poop on the carpet and looks at you as you enter the room, you scoff, "where did that come from?" Your dog looks around the room to help you find the guilty party.

Accountability occurs when a staff member takes ownership of their position and their role on the team. To get that ownership the Leader is going to have to earn the trust of the staff members. The team members are going to watch the leader as much as the leader is going to watch them. The team members want to see if the leader is going to 'walk the talk' or just 'talk the talk'. Trust starts building when the team members see the Leader listening to what they are saying through their spoken and unspoken word:

"The biggest mistake you can make in trying to talk convincingly is to put your highest priority on expressing your ideas and feelings. What most people really want is to be listened to, respected and understood. The moment people see that they are being understood, they become more motivated to understand your point of view." - David Burns (MD and Professor of Psychiatry at the University of Pennsylvania)

Your team members are going to wait to see:

1. If you are going to stand up for them

2. If you are going to give them credit

3. If you are listening to them

4. If you are committed

5. If you hear them

6. If you care

7. How you handle yourself under stress

8. How you handle staff that do not do their work.

9. How you conduct yourself in every situation.

"The important thing to recognize is that it takes a team, and the team ought to get credit for the wins and the losses. Successes have many fathers; failures have none." - Philip Caldwell

One of my favorite quotes about teamwork comes from Harry S. Truman: *"It is amazing what you can accomplish if you do not care who gets the credit."*

When you come onto a unit or into a facility that has been through a lot of changes you have to practice patience. As an effective leader, you are going to have to work through many staff mindsets and apprehensions. As you meet with staff you do not want to open the door to anxiety by asking them what they think are the problems on the unit or in the facility. Instead, you want to ask them to forget what they have been through before you arrived and you want to ask them to clear their minds and leave the garbage at the back door. This is why you take the opportunity to start painting your vision for this unit or facility right up front. When you meet with staff, encourage them to participate in the painting of the unit/facility vision. Let your passion flow and start winning their hearts with getting them involved with the future.

In Wikipedia, in the definition of Accountability it states: "Accountability cannot exist without proper accounting practices; in other words, an absence of accounting means an absence of accountability."

Once a staff member knows what they are accountable for, then the leader has to hold them accountable. Like it or not, you have to stand firm and be fair and equable.

As a 'newbie' manager, I was good at paper compliance because it was easy to read what needed to be done related to accountability; the hard part was when I had to apply what needed to be done when there was no accountability. Geeze! I hated the game of "who me." Rarely did the offending party, own up to their mistake. The majority of the time the guilty party wanted to excuse their behavior and blame everyone else around them for why they did what they did. Accountability meant I had to put on my "parental" hat.

Society has tried for years to soften discipline by giving it another label, but you know what? 'Discipline is discipline'. Call it anything you like; corrective action, re-directive counseling or in-service, but the bottom line is someone did not do what they were supposed to do or they did something they should not have and now someone has to handle it. When a team member has not followed policy or stepped over the line, you need to take action quickly. The longer you wait the worse it will get; you can try to avoid it by putting it in a drawer, but eventually the drawer will explode and then you will have an issue that has morphed into something bigger and uglier. I am going to someday make a billion dollars because I am going to create a vaccine for stupidity and immaturity.

I found the following steps to be very helpful when it comes to disciplining:

• Keep the focus on the issue at hand

• Leave your temper in your hip pocket

• Do not make it personal

• Listen to what they are saying

• Get to the point

• Discuss ownership of the actions taken

• Develop an achievable action plan

• End the meeting

I cannot emphasize strong enough how important "keeping the focus on the issue" is in resolving situations.

I sat with one of my Unit Managers as they discussed with one of her Charge Nurses about missing the administration of a medication to one of their assigned patients. The patient was out walking around after not receiving their medication and fell down with a seizure. The medication that had been skipped was the patient's seizure medication. From the fall the patient received a blow to the head which resulted in several stitches to the forehead.

The only excuse the Charge Nurse gave was that she was having troubles at home and she was distracted by those issues. She was sorry she had missed the medication and the patient was hurt. The Charge Nurse went on and on about her family issues but never accepted she was at fault. She kept blaming her family issues for making her forget. The medication error was the fault of her family issues.

The Unit Manager listened calmly to the Charge Nurse and then finally told her that she was sorry that she was having troubles at home but the issue was she did not perform her duty as a nurse and a patient was injured. Whether her family issues caused her to be forgetful or not, the point is she allowed her family issues to distract her and it resulted in a negative outcome.

This Unit Manager did an excellent job of keeping the focus on the incident without denying the Charge Nurse had issues at home. The Unit Manager held the Charge Nurse responsible for her lack of ability to stay focused while at work on her assigned patients. The Unit Manager reminded the Charge Nurse of the fact that she was a nurse and it was her responsibility to know her mistakes can cause death and her head must be in the game while at work.

The Unit Manager knew her responsibility and she was holding the Charge Nurse accountable. The Charge Nurse complained that we were not being understandable of her situation and that she should only receive a warning for the medication error. The fact that a resident sustained an injury due to her medication error was of no importance to her. How sad!

With each "re-organizer" assignment, I learned something new that helped the next position go more smoothly. My second go around in the hospital, I made certain I had back-up for call-offs. In hospitals, it was easier to get that back-up, but when I switched to the Nursing Home Industry I found that was not a luxury that was going to be afforded me often. But none the less I had to deal with the issue of nurses calling off at the last minute as a game to frustrate me and get me to leave the leadership role.

Filling in on the floor as a nurse or a nursing assistant, after you have worked a full shift, is not a favorite activity of anyone. However, as a leader, if you want to get the point across that you will not put up with anything just so you do not have to work the floor; you are going to have to put your nurse's shoes on once in a while. The testing will only last a season and then you will reap the harvest.

Tips I learned when I was in Long Term Care to help deliver care when nursing staff was low:

1. Talk to the Administrator and ask him/her to require a mandatory work schedule. With a mandatory work schedule, staff is required to come in and work or be disciplined. This is for the wellbeing and safety of the resident.

2. Ask the Administrator to require office staff, social services, housekeeping, activities, therapy, admissions, regional, etc. to help on the floor. These individuals can wheel residents to the dining room, they can help deliver trays, they can make beds, they can wheel or walk residents to the showers (as long as there is not a risk of a fall), they can fill water pitchers, pass snacks, answer call lights and handle the small issues that go with the call light notifications, etc.

3. If it is a multi-facility organization, see if you can post your open shifts that need to be filled in one of the other facilities that may be close by to see if there are staff members who would like to pick up extra time.

4. Before you experience a staffing emergency, make it a facility policy that all staff members be trained as dining and feeding aides.

5. Making the entire facility responsible for the wellbeing of the resident takes away the division of departments and the tendency to operate in separate and uninvolved with each other.

6. Working together also means when dietary personnel are low, nursing will pull individuals in to help in the kitchen well as housekeeping.

7. There is only one reason for anyone to be in health care and that is to make their patients and residents their priority. The residents and patients need us and we are given the honor to care for them.

One evening I was leaving to go home after I had already put in 12 hours, I heard a loud voice by the nurse's station stating she was not going to take that hall. The voice was the voice of a normally very attentive Nursing Assistant. Tonight, she was letting her Charge Nurse know that she did not like a certain resident and she was not going to take that hall, blah, blah. I asked the Charge

Nurse and Nursing Assistant to take the discussion into a room and out of the range of the residents and family members. The Nursing Assistant refused to move. She continued to speak loudly and finally started threatening to leave if she did not get her way. The facility certainly did not need this Nursing Assistant to leave, but the Charge Nurse could not allow the Nursing Assistant to continue to act the way she was currently acting. This behavior could not be condoned, nor could the facility run the risk of this Nursing Assistant taking her frustrations out on the residents.

The Charge Nurse had already mentioned switching certain residents around to different staff members to help solve the issue but this Nursing Assistant was not open to any accommodations being made; in fact, she just became more indignant and bossy. Finally the Nursing Assistant turned and started walking out of the building stating she, "had better things to do this evening than put up with this s_ i _!" This was totally out of character for this Nursing Assistant, and it saddened us all that she was acting this way. The Charge Nurse did exactly what we had said we would do, she looked at the Nursing Assistant and told her that if she walked out she could keep on walking and never come back. The Nursing Assistant shouted back, "Whatever!" The Charge Nurse turned and looked at me; now it was my turn to back up what I had been saying and "walk my talk." I got the pleasure of working as a nursing assistant until 11pm.

The next afternoon, the Nursing Assistant that had walked out the night before came to my office. She apologized for her behavior and could not explain what got into her. She just "cracked" (as she put it). I sat and listened to her. As I listened, I heard no "just cause" for her behavior. I heard a lot of shifting of blame to her home life and she was tired. I told her I recognized that issues at home can affect one's ability to focus at work, but none of her issues were a new development. She agreed. This Nursing Assistant was asking for her job back. I asked her what the team had decided would happen when something like what she did occurred. She knew the consequences but she wanted me to make an exception for her. I told her I wished her luck in her future endeavors, but I was not going to offer her job back. I walked her to the back door of the facility.

"If you don't stand for something, you will fall for anything." - Rev. Peter Marshall -1947

I really liked this nursing assistant, she was excellent with the residents and she knew her position and performed it well. Before this incident she was usually on time and ready to go to work. I was tempted to be swayed, but I knew if I did I would regret it later. There was no excuse for her behavior. As good as she usually was, that night she did not care what was going to happen to the residents. That is a breach of ethics that cannot be condoned.

According to the 2012 Gallup, Inc. survey...

Engaged Employees:

• Lead to more productivity

• Lead to more profitability

• Are more customer/resident-focused

• Are safer

• Are more likely to 'refuse' to accept offers to leave

Disengaged Employees:

• Erode the bottom line

• Break the spirits of colleagues

• Cause injury to both residents/patients and other staff members

• Led to $300 billion in lost productivity

2011 JCFD Survey of Frontline Health Care Employees resulted in the following conclusion:

Key Drivers for Encouraging Employees Engagement:

• Career advancement/development opportunities

• Feeling informed/open communication/concerns listened to and acted upon

• Fair and attainable recognition and rewards system/process

- Understanding Mission/Vision of the Organization

- Appropriate/professional leadership/management behavior

- Collaborative work environment/team atmosphere

- Line of sight between employee performance and organizational mission

- Positive organizational reputation/pride in the workplace

- Trust/integrity of leadership/management

- Leadership/management interest in employee well-being

- Challenging/motivating work assignments

- Resources provided to perform work successfully

- Conduct annual engagement surveys and act upon results

- Proper fit for the jobs

"Employees do not leave organizations, they leave management"

The associates you work with will judge the entire organization that employs all of you by 'your behavior'. If you are fantastic but the organization is not that great, the employees will think the organization is wonderful. If you are a weak supervisor, the employees will see the organization as weak. As a leader, you will define the company.

Employees want to be held accountable, but they also believe a leader should be held accountable. You cannot expect to tell an associate he/she cannot make personal calls while on duty and you repeatedly receive phone calls from your family. If you expect everyone on the unit to answer patient lights, then you should not walk by a room with a light on and not respond. Half the time a light goes on, it is something simple they need; and if it is not simple, you as the manager can get the right individuals to handle the patient's request. Thank God for new technology where patient/resident can now contact housekeeping or dietary directly.

We have discussed discipline, so let's switch gears now and talk about 'spot lighting' associates for doing their job well…! My mama always said you can get more flies with honey than you can with vinegar. If you want staff to engage and stay with the facility or unit, then they need to hear how well 'you' think they are performing their duties and how important 'you' see they are to the team. An employee cannot shine in their position if they do not know their responsibilities and what is expected of them. Therefore, that brings us back to job descriptions and performance expectations. Before a leader can brag, it has to be clear to everyone on the team who is accountable for what!

Employees look for a leader that demonstrates respect, trust and an emotional intelligence. They want a leader that is interested in them and cares about them beyond their role at work.

Employees watch to see if a leader cares to:

1. know their nick-name if they have one and if not, does the leader know what they like to be called. Even I judge my bosses by whether they call me Peg or Peggy. If they call me Peggy, then I know they have not invested in me (Peggy was my mother's name, I am Peg).

2. Know if they have children, pets or both.

3. Know where they derive fulfillment.

4. Know if they are in school to further their education or change fields

5. Know their hobbies, favorite sport team, whether they fish or hunt, crochet, read books, photography, etc.

6. Know their birthdays, anniversaries, etc.

7. Know their spouse or significant other's name.

8. Know their favorite colors, foods, books, plays, movies, etc.

9. Know specific interests…. like traveling to foreign countries.

10. Respect their faith.

"Employees feel a heightened sense of worth when leaders take a few moments to get to know them and learn what is important to them. Employees appreciate hearing they are doing a good job and their contributions are valued. Non-financial elements like appreciation and recognition have the greatest potential to boost engagement." - (Gebauer, 2008)

DuPont Manager, Richard Knowles, when leading a manufacturing plant in a more participatory manner, decided to stop setting goals for people, because he found he always set them too low. He discovered that when people found meaning in their work, he could count on them to donate their 'discretionary energy'. This is the energy, enthusiasm and hard work available, beyond the minimum required to keep a job, when people work in conditions that allow them to find meaning at work. This is the energy organizations want to tap into in order to fully utilize employee engagement for organizations and personal success.

Mr. Knowles instituted self-appraisals and it worked well for him. I also instituted self-appraisals and it worked well. I did not just go in and say we are done with the old appraisals; I first introduced the idea at a staff meeting and then asked for written feedback. After the feedback, we started having meetings and agreed on new expectations. After about 4 months of meetings and tweaks, we did our first trial. There were some speed bumps, but on the whole it went well and continued on until it became the way we always did appraisals.

The feedback we repeatedly received:

• It was agreed that in order to get proper input there had to be clear precise job descriptions and expectations per position

• Staff stated that having input made them think about what and how they were doing their job and if they could do it better

• They said having input let them become the voice, instead of being just the recipient

• Ownership of evaluating their own performance led them to a better understanding of their own strengths and weaknesses

• It helped keep them aware of what was going on in the organization

• They liked that their appraisal became a 'Two-Way' conversation about performance, priorities and challenge

Some other ways to encourage employee engagement are:

1. Appropriate Rewards... to give a reward because you are told to reward someone once a month is as effective as a 'screen door on a

submarine'. Before a true reward can be appreciated the leader must show they know the difference between good performance and poor performance and that they will handle both performances appropriately. Use the employees from all levels of authority to create the criteria and goals for the rewards. They should develop the action plans, approaches and accomplishments that foster and reward based on performance.

• Rewards should be recognized publicly.

• Develop non-monetary rewards so rewards do not diminish when funds reduce.

• Communicate clearly the actions and behaviors the organization values and want replicated.

2. Communication – Clear and Precise! An erosion of trust can take place if staff members do not think their leaders are forthcoming with information. Whether perceived or real, lack of communication triggers uncertainty and makes employees fear the worst. Rumors fly and employees talk and then they involve the public.

• When staff know what they are doing is good, they will keep doing it and many times they will do more of it. Staff craves feedback daily on how they are doing and if what they are doing is worth getting a 'thank you'.

• Staff wait to see if their input is going to be used. On a daily basis you should demonstrate how the staff's feedback is being used.

• Display clear expectations to the staff that the organization has for the leaders and the managers. Leaders need to build trust by ensuring that their words and actions are consistent.

3. Build Trust – Let Go. Delegation is good for leaders because it expands their managerial ability and it is good for the employee because it offers growth potential for him/her. Delegation demonstrates trust to the employee that the leader believes he/she can do the job correctly and in return with that demonstrated trust the employee takes ownership in the task.

Examples of delegation:

• Single out one employee daily to openly praise for something he/she has done right. Do not be vague.

• Send employees out of the building to learn a task or procedure and have them return to train the rest of the staff. This shows you have confidence in them to bring back the right information and pass it on accurately.

• Let an employee make a decision that will affect a process. JCFD survey showed that when employees are not involved in work decisions that directly affect them they may develop the impression that their input is looked upon as ineffectual and of no value.

Use Ideas from all levels…

Herb Kelleher, founder and Executive Chairman of the Board for Southwest Airlines, states:

> *"I've never had control and I never wanted it. If you create an environment where people participate, you don't need control. They know what needs to be done and they do it." He continues, "We're not looking for blind obedience. We're looking for people who on their own initiative want to be doing what they're doing because they consider it to be a worthy objective. I have always believed that the best leader is the best server. And if you're a servant, by definition you're not in control."*

Involve staff and have them contribute their ideas on how things should be done in the nursing department in order for excellent care to be given to the resident/patient. Ownership comes when you are part of the solution. I realize this is not something that can be developed over night, but if you want to quit carrying all the monkeys on your back, then take the first step and ask for solution ideas.

Peer Involvement…

• Include peer staff in the hiring process

• Include peer staff in the writing of the job descriptions

• Include peer staff in the setting of the job expectations

- Include peer staff on feedback of progress of new employees

- Have peer staff take part in corrective action

- Collaborate and share on problem solving

- Include peer staff on the selection process as to who gets additional training for a job well done

"The best executive is the one who has sense enough to pick good men to do what he wants done, and self-restraint enough to keep from meddling with them while they do it." - Theodore Roosevelt

Lessons learned:

To Attain Employee Engagement It Will Require:

1. Effective and positive management.

2. Shared vision – written and visible.

3. Clean communication – remember if you desire a Coke, describe it precisely or you may receive a Pepsi. Close, but not accurate!

4. Accountability – written for all parties involved.

5. Provide training and the proper tools to achieve success. Let go and trust. If you want them to drive a car, just giving them a set of keys, will not cut it or make it happen.

6. Commitment – buy in from all – to include:

- Time
- Attention
- Training
- Equipment/tools
- Expectations
- Accountability defined

What Employers and Leaders Need To Do:

1. Management/leadership personally knowing their employee

2. Letting employees know that their work is meaningful

3. Effective communication from all levels of leadership

4. Challenging work

5. Employees understanding the vision and mission of the organization

6. Proper recognition for good performance

7. Allow employee input at every level

8. Effective team dynamics

9. Fair compensation

10. Provide proper resources to allow employees to effectively perform their job

11. Make employees feel that leadership cares about their wellbeing

12. Know all employees as individuals with names and different interests

• Take action when a wrong has occurred.

• Do not take it personal.

• Keep the focus on the issue at hand.

• Smile through it.

When you have done enough disciplinary actions, you will find it is just a step that has to be taken like any other job duty. Of course that only occurs after you get over the urge to slap some staff upside the head and kick them in the rear. If a resident or patient is hurt, then you really have to fight the urge to lynch the staff members involved.

CHAPTER 9

"Par...tay!"

"To fly you have to let go of the earth."

One evening after I had started my new management role as Head Nurse of the Step-Down Unit in the hospital, I was sitting in my house thinking about my day at work and suddenly I got a vision of myself. I saw myself with both of my feet pushing against the doorposts of a doorway and I was pulling into me all the assignments to be done on the unit. The staff was on the other side of the doorway trying to pull the assignments out of my hands. I could hear myself saying to them, "here you go", but my actions were saying something totally different. I was thinking I was delegating but the more I reviewed my vision, I saw I was only pretending to let go. I gave out assignments but I was going behind everyone checking to see if they got what they were supposed to be doing done and if they did not, I finished up. How was that letting go?

Have you heard the phrase "Monkey on your back?" It means in management that you are taking on everyone's obligations and putting their monkeys on your back. For instance you are walking down the hallway and one of the nurses on the unit comes up to you; they say, "The IV pump at bed 35A is not functioning well!" You say back to them, I will get a hold of maintenance and have them look at it! You have just taken a monkey on to your back. Instead of asking the nurse what she has done to rectify the problem you just took on the issue.

There is no way one person can do all of the assignments in nursing. If that were the case we would not need all the positions. All my talk about responsibilities, vision, our 'why and accountability' and here I was not letting go. It was time for me to grow up, tie my hands, duct-tape my mouth, and let go. Delegation is simply another way of saying, "hold staff accountable and get out of the way."

Many hands get much done.

It was time for me to get 'my par...tay' on, therefore I began to think that letting go at work could not be too different from letting go as a parent with a child. Do you remember the first time you let your son hold his own 'glass' glass or use a fork?

How about when you let your daughter pick out her own clothes for the day? When it was time to leave the house, did you have a little urge to change her clothes? After all, a sun suit might be a little cool in the midst of winter. How about the first time you let your child cross the street alone! All of these things did not just happen over-night, you built up the confidence to trust and let go.

When my youngest son was learning to drive, I was the one that had the privilege of riding with him while he practiced his driving. I found my son did a great job when I was in the car with him and of course this pleased me. He did not tail gate, he did not speed, he did not sway from lane to lane; he used his signals, he paid attention to other drivers, etc. Therefore, when he passed his driver's ED class and got his license, I was confident he would do well and I did not worry about giving him the keys to the car.

My first delegation to him with the car (of course after the typical run to the grocery store for me) was for him to take over the duty of driving himself to school. After all, he had demonstrated his ability to drive well and he had passed his driver's exam... Right? The very first week he had his license, he received a ticket for trying to pass another car while in an intersection. Now what about letting go? Oh I am not through! We discussed his error and grounded him from the car for a week. He had to review the driver's manual and explain to his dad and me what he should have done.

He got the keys back. A week went by and all was well. Another week and all was well. Then the third week! Not so well! He received a ticket for going 40mph in a 30mph area. What does one do when the person you are wanting to delegate to shows the ability to do the job and understands what to do, but blows it? Do you continue to delegate? Will you ever have peace of mind to totally let go?

That is a difficult question! With our son, he had to go to court and the judge restricted his license for three months. There were no more tickets after that second one and his friends labeled him 'old man' as a driver because when the speed said 25mph he went 25mph not 26mph but definitely 25mph. He was not going to lose his license again. There was no 'third time is the charm'.

What if it took three times? Are you willing to put in that time to an employee?

I do not know if any other manager can tell you what to do in these circumstances. This is a decision that can only be made by the individuals involved. There are several factors, however, that you might want to take into considerations:

1. What are the abilities of the employee?

2. What was going on that made them blow it?

3. Was a life threatened?

4. Does the employee express remorse?

5. If you let go again and something happens again, what do you do?

6. Do you have clear objectives written out? Has the employee signed off on them?

7. Is success clearly defined?

8. Is failure clearly defined?

9. Do you have clear ramifications for success and failure?

10. Who will take over the responsibilities if the delegation is not successful?

The same way we cannot pass judgment on parents that appear in our eyes to be too lenient, we cannot pass judgment on managers that appear to be too lenient with their staff. The important points are approach has to be consistent and fair and equally enforced with all employees. It is not easy to let go, which is why supervisors use different levels of letting go while they are learning their staff and building trust in their staff's abilities.

Tannenbaum and Schmidt (1958) and Sadler (1970), did a study which provided an employee involvement continuum that shows the different ways a supervisor evolves and learns to include their employees in the decision process. Each one is different but each one's purpose is to increase the role for the employees and decrease the role for supervisor.

The process goes like this:

First we Tell: The supervisor makes the decision and announces it to staff. The supervisor provides complete direction. This method is applicable when a supervisor is communicating about safety issues, government regulations and for decisions that neither require nor ask for employee input.

Second we Sell: The supervisor makes the decision and then attempts to gain commitment from staff by "selling" the positive aspects of the decision. Selling comes into play when employee commitment is needed, but the decision is not really open to employee influence.

Third we Consult: The supervisor invites input into a decision while retaining authority to make the final decision them self. The key to a successful consultation is to inform employees, on the front end of the discussion, that their input is needed, but that the supervisor is retaining the authority to make the final decision. This type of employee involvement is the one that creates the most employee dissatisfaction if it is not made clear who retains the authority to the people providing input but made clear that the input of the employee is essential to the success of the project.

Fourth we Join: The supervisor invites employees to make the decision with the supervisor. The supervisor considers his/her voice equal in the decision process. This works when the supervisor truly keeps his/her influence equal to that of the others providing input.

Fifth we Delegate: The supervisor turns the decision over to another party. An important step that will help delegation a success is to always build a feedback loop and a timeline into the process. Share "preconceived pictures" of the anticipated outcome of the process so everyone involved is on the same page.

Reference: Tannenbaum, R. and Schmidt, W. How to Choose a Leadership Pattern. Harvard Business Review, 1958, 36, 95-101.

What does delegation really mean? I was pretty sure it did not mean I was to assign duties then follow up behind staff and complete what they did not accomplish.

Delegate - noun |ˈdeligit| - A person sent or authorized to represent others, in particular an elected representative sent to a conference. A member of a committee.

verb |ˈdeləˌgāt| |ˈdelə'gert| |ˈdelıgert| [trans.] - Entrust (a task or responsibility) to another person, typically one who is less senior than oneself : he delegates routine tasks | the power delegated to him must never be misused.

[trans.] send or authorize (someone) to do something as a representative : Edward was delegated to meet new arrivals.

DERIVATIVES: delegable |-gəbəl| |ˈdeləgəbəl| |ˈdelıgəb(ə)l| adjective delegator |-ˌgātər| |ˈdelə'gerdər| noun

ORIGIN: late Middle English : from Latin delegatus 'sent on a commission,' from the verb delegare, from de- 'down' + legare 'depute.'

In healthcare every professional is a person representing orders we have been given to follow out for the well-being of the patient and resident.

When I was training my children to get themselves up for school, I explained to them what was going to take place and what the ramifications were going to be if they did not get themselves up. Nothing goes smoothly the first time around, but I stuck to my guns and soon I never had to worry again about getting the boys up. What a relief! I hated the constant checking and yelling to get up. I thought to myself, I could do this with my staff. I could delegate, what a relief it would be to not have to carry all these responsibilities and to constantly check to see if duties have been performed.

When I read the above definition, I have to admit it did make me a little nervous. To understand that I was still held responsible for the duties being performed by another individual was not what I wanted to her. However, I still believed I had to delegate if I wanted to grow leaders in the staff that worked with me.

I invested in my children and in my students when I taught school because I did not want to add to the world more individuals that did not benefit world. I certainly did not want my children to live off of my husband and me for the rest of their lives. I wanted them to get an education and earn lots of money (of course I wanted them to be happy at what they did, but I figured they could be happy and rich at the same time, right?) and support me in my old age.

To get started, I did what I told you I did with job descriptions and expectations.

1. I met with each staff member independently and told them precisely what was expected of them.

2. I explained what the rewards would be if they were successful

3. I covered what would happen if they were not successful.

4. Not all employees wanted to take on their responsibilities but as a healthcare professional that is not an option.

5. As a team in our department we decided how many steps and chances would be given to each person.

6. If an employee needed more changes, it was decided their case would go before a committee of their peers.

Do you know what happened once I truly let go, delegated and held staff accountable?

• I got to go home at a decent hour

• I got to enjoy days off like the rest of the staff

• I got to take vacations without interruptions (except to say hi)

• I got to contribute time toward purchasing tools that made our jobs easier

• I got to concentrate on staffing needs and make changes

• I got to work on training to improve our professional skills

• Patient satisfaction survey scores improved

• Assignments got accomplished

• More staff understood the regulations

• Ownership to their shifts and to fill their own call-offs

- When I made rounds, the nursing staff bragged about their accomplishments

- When I made rounds, nursing staff told me what they were doing to improve certain conditions

- Zero deficiency federal and state surveys

- Joint Commission survey with commendations

- Company recognition awards for the nursing staff

- Leaders emerged!!!

- Promotions

- Reputation of the facility and unit improved

Lessons Learned:

- Let go and delegate or you will suffocate under the pressure of trying to do everything yourself

- Nothing happens over-night

- Remember you are a leader not an enabler.

- Know your vision, remember 'why' you are doing what you are doing, invest in others, communicate clearly and often and you will make it.

- If you never let go of the steering wheel, you will always have to drive and you will not get to experience sitting in the passenger's seat and enjoy the scenery

- Staff will rise to the level demonstrated by your belief in them

- Give staff the tools along with a road map, and they will get where they are supposed to be

- Others may smirk at you and say negative things about you, but it is up to you to accept their opinion of you or let it roll off your back. Your positive outcomes will speak for themselves.

- Enjoy life, like yourself and 'par…tay'!

CHAPTER 10

Wow... what a trip!

"To see the world through other's eyes is a gift, only given to the open minded."

The last 9 chapters have been my view of management based on my experiences and after putting it all down on paper, I stand even more assured that there is no one way to do anything; not even leadership. Therefore, my advice to you is…Be you, keep an open mind and feed your creative spirit.

Thank goodness Steve Jobs did not settle for 'just' the typewriter. Below are words of wisdom and different views of leadership from managers I have met along my way:

Jodi A. Wilson
President and Chief Operating Officer
Diley Ridge Medical Center

Just as we do with CPR, focus on the ABC's in a new position. Focus on what needs to come first. You may find an associate who is squealing about their personal issues, but if you have quality or regulatory concerns – this is the priority area and deserves immediate attention.

Devote time to building professional relationships with key individuals. I would suggest scheduling time with new peers, with a focus on legal and regulatory. It is great to get to know these teams before you need their help. Ask these teams their roles, and then ask how you - the new manager - can provide increased compliance or teamwork. "What would make my department really great?"

Clarify expectations of your direct one-up report. Recap areas of departmental concerns gleaned from the interview process and verify that these are what your direct report wants you to focus on. "What are the top three areas that would benefit my department?" I would develop action plans and continually provide updates on progress and revisit areas of need.

Ask your direct report of any areas for professional development that they may have uncovered during the interview process. "Which skill set would you want me to further develop to bring additional value to our organization?"

If this person is new to management, I would also caution that decisions may not be made with the speed they would desire.

Nadine Smith,
COO, Ohana Pacific Healthcare Services

Be open to others opinions, listen, don't just hear what your staff has to say but really listen to what they are trying to tell you. Be an advocate for your staff. Know what is going on in your units. Make sure you have routine and consistent meetings with them formal and informal. I used to do some talk story session where I bring in food and meet informally with the individual shifts. Make sure you are available for them. BUILD RELATIONSHIPS early. It is hard to go back and change the staff's perception once they have developed it. Mean what you say and say what you mean….do not beat around the bush or be vague but be open and honest with staff at all times but in a courteous and professional manner.

John Hughes
Nurse Practitioner Student - *(John was Area Vice President with Extendicare Health Services when I first met him and worked with him. He is an outstanding leader who gives his 'all' to any project he is assigned. John bought and ran Flint Ridge Nursing Home until he decided it was time to do something different with his life).*

Treat others as you, yourself, would wish to be treated. I may have gone home with a bruised ego from time to time in observing that, but in the long run, it has never failed to be the best guidance available.

Shelly Szarek-Skodny, CEO
Healthcare Division
Ceres Enterprises, LLC/ Ohio Inns, LLC

Every day ask your manager or direct boss "Is there anything you need from me today", or "Let me bring you up to speed on my department". Daily exits before ending the day are VERY valuable to both parties.

Michael Milbrandt
Regional Vice President of Operations - Altercare of Ohio

Never forget the reason you went to school to become a nurse…. You are there to help people in need of your expertise. Don't get wrapped up or involved with any of the drama or politics we unfortunately see when working with so many different co-workers.

Like any good parent, choose your battles. You're not going to change the world with big heroics or other sweeping changes....You will choose it by helping one life at a time and caring for people. Generally speaking, we do not remember the administrators, superintendent, or principle at school when we were growing up...but we do remember that favorite teacher we had as a child, it was the teacher that paid attention and listened to us....Likewise with nurses, patients don't necessarily remember who changed their bandage or gave them a pill....But they do remember the nurse that took an extra second of their time to LISTEN to them.

Michael A. Cindrich
RN, Independent Healthcare Consultant

The biggest piece of advice I would like to share is to not come off like you know it all. Relax and listen to what is going on around you. Let others talk more than you. You will have your time to share. You did not get to where you are as a leader if you did not know what you were doing. It is not your job to shine; it is your job to help the staff shine.

Kathy A. Head
VP of Human Resources, Extendicare Health Services

Love your nurse aides and treasure what they do. In turn, they will make your life easier.

Kathy Duffus
www.coachthrulife.com, Career and Personal Coach

I've recently read that for the first time ever, there are now 5 generations in the work force, ages 18 to 80. This has never happened before and so now it is extremely important that managers become aware of the gifting of experience, though it varies, of these multiple generations. Boomers can offer the experience of the traditional work place, the acceptance of responsibility, and a strong work ethic. Although the Millennial's (born between 1977-1997) have a reputation for being more demanding and less responsible, which is not true, they can offer technical expertise and social networking skills that is their forte. They are also not apt to stay in a job longer than 18 months because they have been noted as the ADD generation but that just means, in many cases, that they become bored with a job or position and are always looking to be challenged. Generation X has had the desire to leave the traditional methods of the work place for the convenience of a home office and less hands on management in that setting.

There is an older population in the work place as they, who have found retirement to be financially challenging and or not stimulating, have had to return. These are the dependable and steady who are willing to do whatever they can to contribute to an organization.

My advice to a manager would be to nurture their employees and have an open approach to exploring what makes them unique. A manager who can identify the talents of the generational employment pool available and enhance the qualities and experience of variety will be far ahead in their approach.

Debbie Massara
RN, Director of Nursing, Ohana Pacific Health Services

First would be to make decisions based on the needs of the resident. Second is to listen to their staff and be willing to do hands-on care a long side them. And last, but not least is teach their staff every day, because when we know better, we do better!

Christopher Tobin, D.C.
Positive Outcomes Chiropractic Clinic.

I would like to share a lesson I was taught as a teen ager. I was asked to take a paper plate and a tube of toothpaste and squeeze some of the toothpaste onto the paper plate. I was told I could use anything I wanted to put the toothpaste back into the tube. Struggle as I may; I was unable to put all the toothpaste back. Not only could I not get all the toothpaste back in, I also was unable to regain the integrity of the tube once I had squeezed it.

The instructor shared, that words are like toothpaste, once they are 'squeezed' out of the mouth; there is no taking them back. Therefore, if the words are bad you will not be able to put things back the way they were and you will never be able to regain the integrity of the situation.

As a leader use your words to freshen those around you!

Joyce Barrett, CEO
Quilters on the Canal / Board Member of 'A Special Wish Foundation'

As the founder and coordinator of The Quilters on the Canal, one of the most important qualities is to have a caring heart.

Last year, one of my ladies passed away. She had been ill for several months and we all knew that her time was short. She openly shared her thoughts and feelings with us-as well as sharing her amazing stash of quilting fabric, sewing tools and books. It was like Christmas every week when she would wheel in boxes of goodies that she wanted us to have.

After Judy passed away, there was no funeral. The next time our group met, I told them I would have a memorial service for her-it was really for all of us. I read what I had prepared, had a moment of silence and then prayer. I opened the "floor" for anyone who wanted to share and we laughed, shed a few tears and then got our sewing machines out and began the day of sewing that we all love, 'A sewing day that Judy loved, too'.

I have learned many things over the last seven years with this group.

1. I have followed God's plan for this group. He instructed me to not organize the group as a guild (with rules, challenges and dues) but to create/maintain a happy, positive atmosphere. Sometimes this has required me to guide and to correct the topics of conversation.

2. Working with senior citizens can be wonderful and sad at the same time. I allow for those times and am open to their feelings.

3. I looked for a woman (delegation) who would be able to open and set up for the sewing day when I was not able to be there. Sharyn arrives on time, helps set up the equipment without being asked, frequently asks "what can I do?" and is always eager to give a helping hand.

4. I have taken note of each woman's area of expertise and level of ability. If someone is having trouble with a hand quilting stitch, I can encourage the best hand quilter to give a mini lesson. This has happened without my even asking. There is an atmosphere of freedom where any member can call out for help and there are always several who jump at the opportunity to give a hand.

5. I take time to know each woman and her situation.

6. I keep an updated birthday/address/email list. It helps to keep them connected.

7. Each woman has a "tent" type name card at her machine.

What has evolved is a quilting/sewing group that cares for one another, takes shopping and quilts show trips together, plans potlucks, attends funeral home visitation together, sends cards to each other and puts on the nicest quilt show during the town's festival.

Recently, we had a Saturday evening quilt show. As we were taking down the quilts, Carol said, "Oh, we get to come back in only two days and sew again!!" For this divorced senior, our quilting day is the highlight of her week!

Pamela Lemasters
Admissions Representative, Fortis College (School of Nursing)

The most important thing I would want a new nurse manager to know (or any new manager for that matter) is that he or she already possesses the skills, knowledge and abilities to get the job done. This is not the time to show off skills; rather this is where the rubber meets the road with regard to matters of the heart. It is about doing the right thing all the time. It is about making decisions based on what is right instead of what is better to get ahead. As long as he or she does not allow impaired judgment to make decisions, the success will be limitless.

Diane Stewart, RN
VP of Operations, Golden Living

• Do not get drawn into drama with peers or subordinates and do not be a drama generator.

• Let your staff learn to trust you by you being trustworthy, always.

• Take the high road in any ethically ambiguous areas. If a decision feels "icky" then it almost certainly is the wrong decision.

• Surround yourself with good people.

• Trust your instincts.

• Be a consistent and fair communicator.

• Be willing to roll up your sleeves and work side by side with staff. Nothing is worse for morale than a leader sitting in an office or in a meeting when the staff is swamped with work.

• It doesn't matter what religion you are, or if you have no religion, the Golden Rule is a universal truth, treat others as you wish to be treated.

• Look in the mirror, at least once a week, and ask these questions: What value have I brought to my job, work, employer, supervisor, co-workers, patients, etc.? What could I have done better? What did I do well?

Sandra Mclellan, RN
Nurse Consultant

Respect your elders - and I don't just mean the residents and patients. The mature members of your staff will doubt your ability just because of your age. Ask for their help and advice. It will build trust.

Do what you say you are going to do - and do it before the time you said you would. It will build trust.

Wear a smile and be kind. You may be "in charge", but don't act like it. Save the "in charge" part for when you have to make a critical decision, not day to day behavior. Be fair and consistent so your team knows what to expect from you.

Always be open to new opportunities. Never turn down an interview. Invest an hour or so of your time learning about a new position and meeting someone you may network with later. Save ALL your business cards and don't change your cell or home phone number unless you have to. Someone may call you years later with the perfect opportunity!

Keep your personal opinions, especially negative ones, about your team-mates to yourself. You never know who is related to whom, or in a "special" relationship.

Don't hire relatives unless it's your whole staff. You will always be suspected of favoritism, even if it's not true.

Don't mix your love life and your work life. Quit the job or quit the relationship.

Don't give your staff a reason to gossip about you. Keep your personal life to yourself. Family and friend photos on your desk are enough to let them know you have some.

Don't socialize too personally with people who report to you, and never overuse alcohol. You can get to know them just fine over lunch or at a picnic table. You don't want them to think you are one of them...you're NOT!

Respect your boss. They sign your checks. If you make a mistake, (and you will), admit it and apologize. It will build trust.

William Tobin, CFO
Tobin & Associates, Inc.

If you want to keep associates loyal, practice what you speak:

1) Tell the truth. Be transparent and you will not have to worry about back peddling.

2) Communicate expectations: You would not want anyone to surprise you with bad news, therefore, do not surprise your associates. Make sure you understand where they are coming from and that they understand where you are coming from. Make a plan and stick to it as a team

3) Value associates. Care for the people you work with and do not play games with their emotions. No one likes to be played.

4) Be fair, open and responsible. Accept your responsibility as a leader and act with integrity, commitment and honesty.

5) Create a culture where 'manure' is not the only fertilizer used to develop an individual's strengths and talents.

I began my adult career as a teacher of high-school students with learning disabilities; this is where I discovered I had a passion for helping others achieve. I explored a new dimension of my passion when I became a registered nurse (RN) at the age of 40. My professional nursing career has opened doors for me to work in the areas of Sub acute, Long Term Care, Med Surg, ICU, Telemetry, Outpatient Clinics and Case Management.

I shared earlier in the book about my career as a Director of Nurses in Long Term Care Facilities; therefore, I will not repeat it again. As a Corporate Nurse in the Reimbursement Division, I lead a team of nurses to re-capture 8 million dollars of suspended Medicare dollars for one district and the 'recapturing' trend continued for 6 other districts. As Corporate Nurse, I was given the assignment to operate in the capacity of a company representative for several Administrative Law Judge Hearings regarding Medicare CMS Denial Cases. My experience as a nurse helped me win every case assigned to me in favor of the Company.

Being a nurse manager has allotted me the privilege to teach nurse managers how to develop staff and administrators how to develop facility teams.

When I joined Geri-Nurse in 1998, it had been struggling financially for some time. It was so bad I thought I had made a stupid mistake and started to look for other positions. But to be honest the financial picture was not the real reason I went looking so quickly. I missed the corporate world and I dearly missed not having a corporate title. Little 'ole' me had gotten caught up with titles and now that I was a no body with no territory to oversee, I did not think I had any worth. That is why I went looking; I wanted validation that I was still important and I went looking for that validation in a title.

I found an organization that was willing to work with my limited ability to travel and I made it to the 6th and final interview, before I woke up. I sat in the reception area waiting to meet with the CEO and I became sick to my stomach. It dawned on me as I sat and watched all the 'suits' come and go out of the CEO's office, that this was really not what I wanted. I had been given a wonderful gift at Geri-Nurse and I was about to blow it. At Geri-Nurse, I could set my own schedule and I had a say on how things would go in the organization. I may not have been what the industry called a 'big shot' but I had something I had never had before in a position; I had freedom. If I went with large organization, I would have a VP title again but my voice would again become a voice among many other voices.

I cannot tell you why it took me so long to appreciate Geri-Nurse, but once I did wake up; I went back to Geri-Nurse with renewed energy and a determination to make it a success. Within three months of my decision, the bottom line went from red to black. The owner was so floored that he offered me the opportunity to purchase Geri-Nurse. I thought on that offer for a while and after long conversations with my husband, a longtime healthcare executive, and our eldest son, we decided to gamble everything and purchase Geri-Nurse. We figured if it didn't work out, we could fall back on our professional credentials.

Fortunately, for all of us there was no falling back! We recognized the limitations of Geri-Nurse, which focused on placing RNs, LPNs [licensed practical nurses] and CNAs [certified nursing assistants] in local facilities and thought, if we could shift the focus to placing healthcare executives, then we could go nationwide and operate in a field we were more familiar. We changed the business model, changed the name to Tobin & Associates and went national in 1999 and our company has become a trusted name in executive healthcare recruitment.

Even though I was very pleased with the success of Tobin & Associates; I thought I should do more; therefore, my husband and I develop Conceptual Beginnings Ltd., in 2004. Conceptual Beginnings is an investment company which we use to financially support micro startup companies. In 2006, I co-founded Interactive Care Network (ICN) with Andy Figallo; ICN is a web based application currently located in hospitals at the bedside of the patients. This application assists the patient and their family members to locate after-hospital care services. In 2012, I established a non-profit organization which is designed to develop successful leaders, 'Ordinary People Make A Difference'.

And you know what? 'I AM NOT DONE YET!'

IN CLOSING

Through my eyes!

"Give life your best and when your day is done;
a smile will dress your face."

The sun rays were shining through our front windows and deflecting off the crystal vase creating quite a kaleidoscope of colors in the living room. I was mesmerized by its' beauty. As much as I needed to concentrate on getting things packed for our big move, I was finding it hard to focus. I reached over to the coffee table and picked up a gift my eldest son had given to me when he was six years old.

In a flash, I was transformed backwards in my mind. I saw myself leaning against the railing on the front porch of our first home. I was watching my spirited 6 year-old, Marty, gingerly step off the bus. His normal bounce had been replaced with very precise steps. He had asked me to be on the front stoop today when he arrived from school. He said he had "some-ting" special for me.

Marty was the type of child that soaked in every event in his life as if it was the very nutrient that gave him existence. He never greeted you with a hello, that he did not accompany it with a smile and an action that let you know you had been greeted loud and clear.

Most little boys brought their mothers dandelions; Marty brought me dead rats from the woods. He thought dead rats were really, really neat because they had teeth and nails and everything.

On this day as I watched him bring me his "some-ting" special, I was a little apprehensive as to what Marty would call special. I could see his gift was wrapped in bright yellow tissue paper and every possible area that could be open was sealed tight with scotch tape.

Finally he had made it to the stoop; he stood in front of me, with his arms straight and reaching up. His body stood as if he was at attention except for his arms. His blue eyes twinkled as he waited for me to take my gift.

I carefully took the gift and went inside. I sat on the couch and pulled at the wrapping. It took a while but finally, the gift was exposed. Marty stood in front of me with every pore in his body oozing with excitement for my response. I smiled, put my arms around him and kissed his cheek. I had absolutely 'no clue' what his brown ceramic creation represented.

With complete and unabashed admiration, Marty took his craft and put it in the center of the coffee table. As he stood there gazing at it, he said, "Mommy, don't you think that is the neatest lizard you have ever seen?" I smiled and chuckled silently. I looked at him and agreed. Here I was again, experiencing life and beauty through the unique eyes of my six year old son. Other mothers that day received bird houses and saucers but not me, I received a lizard.

For years, every time I would move his lizard creation to the book shelf, Marty would move it back to the coffee table and say, "Mom you forgot to move my lizard back to the coffee table when you dusted, but I took care of it for you, no problem!" I smiled as I continued to reflect back on those days and carefully packed the lizard for the move to our new home.

As I came back to reality, I heard in the distance a truck. I looked out the front window and saw Marty driving up the street, all grown up and in his 4 x 4 truck. There he was with the same twinkling blue eyes and enjoying every bouncing motion of his truck. My little blond hair boy had grown up and now had children of his own.

I no longer received ceramic lizards or dead rats, those types of gifts had given way to practical things like gift certificates and perfume. The other change was now Marty moved his lizard creation to a shelf on the bookcase and it was me that move it back to the coffee table. To Marty that ceramic lizard had become a silly childhood memory with very little meaning. However, to me it had become the opposite, that little lizard had taken on more and more meaning as the years passed and my little boy grew up.

Time came and time went, dust settled and dust was swept away. But my gift became clearer and clearer to me:

Marty's brown ceramic creation in my eyes was my little blue-eyed, blond hair six-year old boy reaching his arms up to his mommy and giving her one of the most precious gifts of her life, "a part of him".

Someday I may make another move and it may be to a nursing home and if this should happen, I will take my ceramic creation with me. Therefore, dear nurses, when I can no longer do for myself... please remember what I see when I look at this creation... and please treasure it for me.

Recommendations:

Tracy A. Imhoff, LNHA
Kindred Healthcare Services - worked indirectly with Margaret (Peg) at Tobin & Associates and Interactive Care Network

"I have been a friend of Peg Tobin for several years. However, before I was her friend, I was acquainted with her expertise. Peg is well known in the health care industry for her training as a clinician, her gifting as a teacher and instructor, and her practical "down to earth" style and it is that style that has Peg Tobin in high demand from the facility level to the state and national levels. Her knowledge and wisdom come from many years of education, hard work, and determination that have made her successful as a floor nurse, director of nursing, regional consultant, corporate consultant, business owner and entrepreneur. Every time I have a conversation with Peg, I feel I come away having learned something I didn't know before. If you have never met her, I urge you to get to know Peg Tobin through this book. Read her thoughts, open your mind to her experience and learn from her instruction. As you converse with Peg through her writings, I know that you will also come away having learned things that you didn't know before."

Lee Ann Kaut, Resource Specialist/Recruiter
Tobin & Associates - worked directly with Margaret (Peg) at Tobin & Associates

"Margret (Peg) Tobin is a dedicated employer who cares deeply about her staff. She displays true professionalism and is a leader who displays strong ethics and integrity. It is a pleasure to be a part of her firm and a privilege to be associated with her company. I strongly recommend Peg Tobin and Tobin and Associates."

Melissa Fisher, Lead Strategist / Principal
Fisher4Marketing LLC - was with another company when working with Margaret (Peg) at Tobin & Associates

"Peg is wonderful to work with, and she is a gifted leader for her business and for the healthcare industry. She has committed her life's work to helping people, including employees, candidates, and those in need of direct care. Her enthusiasm, quick laugh, and can-do spirit are surpassed only by her extensive healthcare industry knowledge. Anyone fortunate enough to work with her should listen intently, learn quickly, and be prepared to be inspired."

Billijean Ball, Nurse Manager
Friendship Village of Columbus - reported to Margaret (Peg) at Tobin & Associates and Interactive Care Network

"I have had the privilege to work with Peg on two separate occasions in two different positions. I love working with her because she helps you grow into the best worker you can be, she stimulates her coworkers by teaching them to think for themselves and encourages them with laughter and praise. I would follow her anywhere if she would remain my boss."

Larry Trimmer, Owner
Trimmer Financial Services - was a consultant or contractor to Margaret (Peg) at Tobin & Associates and Interactive Care Network

"Peg is an executive who leads by example. Peg treats her employees the way she would want to be treated. Peg watches her financials and knows how to motivate her employees when tough times are noted. She has grown her company from a handful of employees to nearly a couple dozen in the last five years. Peg is someone everyone should know."

Sara Rose, President / Attorney
Sara L. Rose, LLC - was a consultant or contractor to Margaret (Peg) at Tobin & Associates and Interactive Care Network

"I have had the opportunity to work with Peg for quite some time now. I always find her to be organized, competent and hands-on. Her attention to detail and professionalism even in difficult situations has impressed me. Peg's dedication to her work is reflected in the growth of and the ingenuity involved with her businesses."

Jill Thomas, RNC, Owner
Advance Care Planning, Inc. AND Clinical Compliance Concepts,
Inc. worked with Margaret (Peg) at Tobin & Associates and
Interactive Care Network

"Peg and I have similar companies and we are friendly competitors. At times we assist each other with resources. Peg is fair and honest and I am never concerned about her or the integrity of her company. In addition, she is a wealth of knowledge in our industry Long Term Health Care.

William Arnett, Development Director
Fairfield County - was with another company when working with
Margaret (Peg) at Tobin & Associates and Interactive Care
Network

"Margaret (Peg) Tobin is an outstanding business executive. She is a results-oriented leader with the highest levels of integrity and ethics."

Lisa Stevens [LION 2900+], Senior Director
Act II Resources. - reported to Margaret (Peg) at Tobin &
Associates and Interactive Care Network

"I have worked with (and for) Peg Tobin for over 6 years. Her personal experience and understanding of the LTC industry is unparalleled. Peg is a both a critical thinker and visionary and she has been an invaluable mentor and resource to me."

Steve Biondi, VP Clinical Services
Extendicare - managed Margaret (Peg) indirectly at Tobin &
Associates and Interactive Care Network.

"Peg is one of the brightest and most talented nurse leaders that I have had the pleasure of working with in my health care career. She is energetic, able to solve problems, and always a professional. I highly recommend working with Peg."

Abby Katz
PNC – Business Banking– involved with Margaret 'Peg'Tobin
through Tobin & Associates, Interactive Care Network,
Conceptual Beginnings, and Ordinary People Make A Difference.

"It is an honor to know and be involved with Peg Tobin. She is one of the most inspiring and successful businesswomen I have ever met. My hope is to someday to achieve a portion of the success she has in her life. I have been fortunate to attend one of Peg Tobin's presentations and observe her in action; I have never seen a speaker interact so well with her audience and get them all to participate. Her topics and presentations are very motivational and what she shares is applicable to every person in that room!"

Darrell Donalds , Technology Manager
Tobin & Associates

I have had the privilege of getting to know Peg over the last 6 months. Her expert knowledge and experience, combined with her honesty and integrity, make working with her a pleasure. I am very impressed with her leadership skills and the way she brings out the best in people. Her creative ideas and enthusiasm for success are inspirational and I look forward to her guidance for years to come!

Made in the USA
Lexington, KY
06 December 2017